THIS IS SOCIAL MEDIA

How to Tweet, Post, Link and Blog Your Way to Business Success

Guy Clapperton

CAPSTONE

This edition first published 2009
© 2009 Guy Clapperton

Registered office
Capstone Publishing Ltd. (A Wiley Company), The Atrium, Southern Gate, Chichester, West Sussex, PO19 8SQ, United Kingdom

For details of our global editorial offices, for customer services and for information about how to apply for permission to reuse the copyright material in this book please see our website at www.wiley.com.

Library of Congress Cataloguing-in-Publication Data

Clapperton, Guy.
  This is social media : tweet, blog, link and post your way to business success / Guy Clapperton.
     p. cm.
  Includes index.
  ISBN 978-1-906465-70-4 (pbk. : alk. paper)   1. Internet marketing.   2. Social media–Economic aspects.
3. Online social networks–Economic aspects.   I. Title.
  HF5415.1265.C577 2009
  658.8'72–dc22

                                                                                    2009031398

A catalogue record for this book is available from the British Library.

Set in 10/15pt Akkurat Light by Toppan Best-set Premedia Limited
Printed in Great Britain by TJ International

CONTENTS

PREFACE

Let me start by annoying you a bit.

We all hate authors who do that. Some sort of smug statement about how clever they are, followed by some waffle about how they've spotted something clever that none of the other authors in their field has even come close to suspecting. It's deeply annoying. I understand that. I get it, really.

Only, I've got this Jaguar. And I've got it because I'm on Twitter.

Well, I say, 'I've got this Jaguar'. Actually, it's a loan for a weekend, but it's free of charge. And the reason it's arrived is because some idiot wrote off my car, I mentioned it on Twitter and Jaguar, bless them, got in touch.

(I'm going to pause this anecdote before people get excited: in this illustration, business owners should bear in mind they're Jaguar, not the lucky bloke who got to borrow a luxury car for nothing. OK, as you were.)

My car was written off at 4 o'clock one morning while it was parked because an uninsured gentleman went into it at speed. These things happen. So I logged onto Twitter, a social network you're bound to have heard of by now, and mention the incident. 'Anybody fancy giving me a free car?' I joked.

Then Jaguar's digital PR got in touch. They couldn't give me a car, they explained (and looking at the insurance costs I can only admit

I'm relieved), but they would be pleased to lend me one in the short term once they've found out a bit more about me. Found out about me? Well, yes. This is social networking rather than an old-fashioned customer/supplier relationship. That's how you build up a relationship with a customer.

Jaguar has used social networking to establish not only its latest vehicles – the XF and XK – but its own identity as an informed, modern company that uses social networks. UK PR manager Nick O'Donnell explained that the aim is to cascade information and indeed emotion about the cars and the brand throughout the various websites and networks available. 'The first phase was to understand who we wanted to reach – and what messages we wanted to get to them. It is as important to communicate information and emotion about our new vehicles to existing and new/potential customers as it is to communicate the change in the brand to the widest possible audience. We aim to challenge some negative perceptions about the brand and influence buyer peer groups. If your peer group regards Jaguar as an older person's car, then this could be the difference between purchase and walking away; we need to get the decision-maker *and* their peers thinking differently about Jaguar and the cars we make,' he says. 'The next phase was how to reach them; so we looked at which websites, blogs and forums could reach these different audiences, and the creator/influencer individuals within these sites that we should communicate with. We looked at motoring, luxury, lifestyle, gadget and technology websites. The plan was to engage with the online individuals that are creating content and discussion on these websites and facilitate them hosting our content and/or help them create their own content about Jaguar (in much the same way as I would do for a print journalist).

'We also identified that the motoring websites and forums (obviously well known to us already as these are led by our off-line contacts, e.g. Top Gear, Auto Car etc.) were responsible for a huge amount of content and discussion about Jaguar across the web,' he continues. 'A focus has been on encouraging Jaguar content and discussion on these sites and maximizing SEO for this activity. For example, there are a huge number of searches for heritage Jaguars – we therefore offer these motoring sites the opportunity to video an old Jaguar alongside a current model.' This sort of engagement is a thousand miles from the traditional approach taken by established motoring brands.

So, why am I telling you this? Well, suppose you'd been a car dealer on Twitter. Suppose you'd seen my moan – or anyone else's – after an accident like that, and you'd stepped up to help. Let's pretend I'm not writing a book so you don't get mentioned in here: that's aiming a little high and only a tiny minority can hope to get into something like that. But I'm complaining about someone having demolished my car, so you drop me a note offering a deal on a replacement. And you follow up with good service, and I follow up with a message on Twitter – or Facebook, or MySpace, or wherever – saying what an excellent company you have. My 2,000 followers on Twitter have just had a free testimonial about your business delivered to their inbox.

A quick reality check, though. Not all of those 2,000 readers will actually see every message I put up on Twitter. Not every one of them will be wanting a replacement car, and you can't be certain that those who are aren't on the other side of the world. But it's another possible chance of getting some business.

Not sold on the idea yet? OK, how about a little market testing to pass the time? It's well known that there are a lot of celebrities on Twitter. Broadcaster Jonathan Ross is one of them. He used the system to set up a book club. He'd been on for about six months and picked up about 200,000 followers, and one day he just announced the club.

Wouldn't it be good, he suggested, if we all agreed to read a book each week and discuss it with these little micro-blogs, or 'tweets', at an agreed time on Sundays?

People responded immediately – great idea, what shall we read – and in May 2009 the Wossy Book Club was born. A trite example? Well, maybe. Richard and Judy had just announced they were going to retire from television, so there was an obvious gap in the market. Did Ross have this in mind at the time? I don't know, I tweeted him about it and didn't get an answer. But that doesn't matter for the moment. He'd built up his followers and he was able to market test an idea in minutes. Think about how long it takes you to consider a new service or product, test it and get it to market.

The bad news is that you're (probably) not Jonathan Ross. Or Ashton Kutcher, or Stephen Fry, or any of the other famous people who have already mastered and become stars of the new medium. They were stars already and they're going to attract a lot of followers precisely because of that.

This ought to be good news for you, though. You don't want to be followed by that many people. Suppose you had 200,000 people reading your posts and the standard 3 percent (if you're doing a flier) decided to wanted to see you. That's 6,000 personal visits from you as a consultant – which is too many, you're unlikely to be able to make those targets. But you might be able to if you had interest from 2,000 people. Or you might be able to retain 200 people as a customer base much more effectively if you had an additional way of keeping in touch with them, something they enjoyed and was cheap to do. By now, the more commercially minded reader should be starting to notice a trend. This social media thing increases people's profits. It makes money, sometimes for everyone except the people behind the social networking website itself.

It can also be royally messed up. If someone misunderstands the medium or, worse, allows their prejudices rather than solid market research to govern who they target and who they don't with their social networking, then it can be a disaster. You want to target teenagers through Facebook? Fine, there are many teenagers on there: but bear in mind that the largest group of people on that network are aged 35–55 (in fact that's the largest constituency on any of these 'teenage fads', as someone once described them to me). We'll be looking in this book at avoiding that sort of mistake.

Probably the easiest way to demonstrate how to do it right, arrogant though this is going to sound, is to tell you a little about how I came to write this book. I joined Twitter in February 2008. I know because it says so on my Twitter Profile and they're very good at recording dates. The only thing is, I didn't really use it until about the following November. You might be the same: signed up, frowned at it, thought about how likely it is that someone else will be remotely interested in what you had for breakfast, signed out again. Frowned a bit more.

I don't know what it was that drove me back in November. I'd been using Facebook as a way of keeping in touch with people, FriendsReunited had been fun while it was attracting new members and putting me back in touch with old mates and LinkedIn had actually produced a tiny amount of work, although most of the people on it were more inclined to show off about how many 'friends' they had than to do anything constructive.

Twitter, however, was starting to make news. Granted, the news was mostly about celebrities using Twitter; the aforementioned Ross, Fry and Kutcher, Philip Schofield, Andy Murray, many of whom raised the system's profile beyond anything its founders could have imagined.

So I went on again and started following some people I knew. I started making little announcements, or tweets as they would be called, myself. And I noticed something. If I mentioned, for example, that I was off media training – training spokespeople to talk to journalists like me without getting tongue-tied or waffling too much, basically – then very often people would hire me again and offer more work because they'd seen me on Twitter talking about what I was doing.

This, I reasoned, was a good game. The Jaguar (sorry, did I mention that again?) helped with that general impression.

Other things started to happen. Editors I was following started to follow me back. For 'editors' you could read 'clients'; I'm a journalist but I could have been anyone trying to sell a service. They started to notice me and come to me when they needed things written. They'd put notes out when they were short of copy. There was, in fact, a very good reason for me to be on Twitter and to continue to be there.

Let me tell you how I secured the contract to write this book. As well as going through the usual channels – approaching agents, sending a synposis to publishers, that sort of thing – I put a note out on Twitter. 'Would anyone be interested in publishing a book on Twitter for business?' I asked. I'm still awaiting replies to the formal book pitches, but within two hours of my putting my initial tweet out, I had a letter from a man in Oregon who was publishing director of John Wiley & Sons, a major business publisher. He referred me to the UK branch of the same company, which passed the idea to its publishing arm for small business, Capstone. No, they weren't interested in doing anything that was so much about Twitter that it ignored the rest; however, they would be very interested if I could do something about social media overall.

You're holding the result in your hand. It's fitting somehow that a book on social media networking happened because the author was able to network with the most likely publisher outside the more traditional route. And of course, several of the interviewees whose input has been invaluable were found through Twitter, Facebook, Blellow, LinkedIn, that sort of thing. By the time you finish you'll know the names and will probably be able to guess which networks I used and which I didn't.

It would be wrong to overstate the role the networking played, though. Something I'll be keen to stress throughout the book is that the technology as a medium is part of the mix, not the whole thing. So yes, I made my initial contact for the book through Twitter and OK, I kept up some of my contacts with the sales team and publicists at the publishers through LinkedIn and other networks. But I also emailed in the proposal for the book as a Microsoft Word document. I met the publisher personally, we shook hands and drank some excellent coffee.

I had coffee with the digital people at Jaguar, come to think of it. Met an actual person. Had proper conversations. My point is that there are already people out there who think digital media and social networking in particular are substitutes for, not useful additions to, a business plan and traditional sales routes. This is plain wrong. It has to be part of, not the whole of, a strategy.

And 'strategy' is an important concept in this book. We'll be focusing loads on planning, on building ideas into something coherent, on justifying costs and ensuring a return on investment. We'll be looking into real costs rather than just the headline prices: Facebook doesn't cost anything to join, but you'll be paying yourself or someone else for the time they spend uploading things, typing facts into it, working out social media promotions. This is a business book, so you need the real costs, not the watered-down stuff that leaves you short of resources and time and nobody has told you why.

But this is getting negative again. Let's consider a few more people other than me and celebrities who have secured business through social media. Simon Apps, for example, is a professional photographer specializing in images for the PR community. He's picked up work by making himself known on Twitter. 'Not thousands of pounds worth, but it's work we wouldn't have otherwise had. And on the basis that once a client has used us, they carry on using us for the foreseeable future, it's definitely worth the investment in time. Besides, I enjoy being able to twitter on,' he says. Interestingly, he's taken the decision – we'll come on to this sort of stuff later – not to talk only about his business when he's online. 'I think it's very important to tweet about everything you do as a person and develop relationships with people. For example, I stalk deer. When I first started on Twitter I had to make the decision whether to even mention it, but it's a big part of what I do so I went for it, but keep my tweets fairly tame when I do mention it and avoid going into the gory bits!'

Vegetarians will no doubt be throwing this book across the room by now, but Apps' decision is a telling one. This is social networking not sales networking, not networking for marketing. Not every contact is going to contribute to sales and not every post or contribution should be made with selling in mind. People buy from people, not companies, and in social media they really need to feel that this is happening.

Ben LaMothe is another interesting case: he has a job, like many people, but he found his job through Twitter. He emailed just before this book was published – on deadline day, in fact: 'Tomorrow I'm starting as a part-time web/social media consultant at United Business Media. This is a job I would not have gotten were it not for

Twitter. I'm not sure who followed whom first, but it started with John Welsh. I had been reading what he was tweeting about – mostly new media and publishing – and decided to throw caution to the wind and ask if he took on any interns. He ended up offering to let me shadow him for a day.

'During that day I met with some of his colleagues, sat in on a meeting he was conducting with the entire editorial staff about blogging, and then went into a meeting with the promotions people in another sector. They wanted to know how to best utilize Twitter to promote an event. John and I talked them through different methods. During that day I also sat briefly at the desks of *The Publican* and *Travel Trade Gazette*.

RT – Retweet – when someone repeats something you've said on Twitter to share it with all their Twitter contacts.

'This was in December. Back then (hard to believe that qualifies as 'back then', but Twitter is fast evolving) it was fairly simple to find the people you wanted to follow. What happened before the job shadow is John RTd some of my tweets. As a result I ended up being followed by some of his colleagues. So I walked into the meeting and was instantly recognized by people I'd never met before. It was all Twitter. One of the people I met was Phil Clarke, who heads a number of construction and sustainable development titles. We shook hands and did introductions.

'The day ended and I returned to my degree. But I sensed there was an additional opportunity. During my time at the TTG desk it was suggested that I should contact them about a week-long internship of sorts. So I did that. A few weeks later I was at the TTG desk as an intern, doing stories, filing online, etc. And on my lunch break I ran into Phil again. This time he had something on his mind. He said he might have a job for me, if I was interested. I definitely was. He didn't have all the details, because it was coming into form at the time. Then we dropped it and didn't speak about it again until I sent him a

DM – Direct message – a Twitter message that can be seen only by the intended recipient.

DM on Twitter asking about the opportunity. That led to more emails and a meeting. Then we had a final meeting where I was formally offered the position.

'I realize it sounds a bit convoluted, but without Twitter I never would have met any of these people, had any of those professional experiences or been offered this job.'

As I was typing that very paragraph, British Telecom announced that it had signed 100 companies to its BT Tradespace scheme, which offers an online shop front to companies and businesses, after Twittering about it just once. Journalist and broadcaster Kelly Rose Bradford uses both Twitter and Facebook: 'As a journalist I've used Facebook and Twitter extensively for putting calls out for case studies, alerting PR people to my needs for stories etc., and for flagging up my work once it goes to print. The advantage of Twitter over Facebook for securing case studies or quotes is the re-tweeting – you have a potentially limitless audience for your original message if your contacts re-tweet it for you.

'I've also had unsolicited work via Twitter – my local community radio station followed me on there because they knew me as a newspaper columnist, but had no idea I also did broadcasting – they found my personal website via Twitter, listened to some sound clips I had on there, and subsequently offered me a weekly slot at their station.

'I've recently set up a second Twitter account which I am going to use as a marketing tool for my forthcoming book and tweet extracts ahead of its release. It's hard to imagine promoting oneself without using social media sites these days, so much so I'm having my business cards reprinted with my Twitter and Facebook user names on – I would truly be lost without them, and think for anyone in business, Twitter in particular is an essential tool.'

Gardening products company Wiggly Wigglers uses a lot of social media, including Facebook and podcasting. It does well out of the podcasts, its staff tell me, because of their shelf life. 'Podcasting has enabled us to develop a 'one-to-many' conversation, which the listener experiences as a one-to-one conversation (usually through their headphones),' said the company in its entry to a business competition (which it won). 'The blog and Facebook group have supported this activity and developed to be a vital part of our feedback loop, enabling us to react to positive and negative concerns quickly and easily. We were the first UK gardening company to podcast and have gained a considerable competitive advantage of having instant searchable entertaining and informative answers to our customer's questions.' The best thing is that they are still finding that people download two-year-old podcasts: how much of your company's advertising still pays its way after such a long time?

This kind of benefit starts with word getting around. It starts with people being allowed the chance to feed back.

This is social media.

INTRODUCTION: THE BACKDROP TO SOCIAL NETWORKING

If you want a book that's going to tell you to get into social media for the sake of it, put this one back on the shelf. It isn't for you. If you want to read a book eulogizing or even evangelizing a particular technology, forget it: this isn't it. My aim is to inform you what's out there in terms of social media and help you assess what it can do for your business, then how to integrate the idea into your work. The first step is always to think about your own customers and how they're going to interact with you ('interact' does sound like jargon but in this case it fits). Do they walk in and talk to you? Phone, email, write?

Don't get me wrong, I'm itching to tell you how other people have used social media to colossal advantage. I can certainly tell you how to sign up for the various flavours of network you can join, and by the time you've finished the third chapter you'll know which one's which. As we go to print, Facebook is the biggest and Twitter has the highest profile, mostly due to a load of celebrities getting involved on both sides of the Atlantic. YouTube is the one that lets you put videos up, as does Bebo, but that's primarily aimed at a younger audience. We'll go into more depth later on, when I'll tell you all about these networks, how they started up and indeed how their aims have changed over the years. And I can point you to ways of matching networks to your business needs. A lot of books make the assumption that you *must* sign up for these things, but frankly I don't accept that. When such networks are right they can work spectacularly. When they're not, they don't.

Another issue with writing a definitive guide to social media is that the landscape changes, and it changes really quickly. Twitter is currently flavour of the month so it crops up a lot in the preface. If I'd been writing three years ago I'd have been telling you about this odd new idea where you put up a really brief summary of exactly what you're doing at the moment – right now – and through which your friends and family can keep in touch. Nowhere was there any idea of two-way conversation, Twitter was a series of announcements and that was it. Fast forward to the present day and we find that users have taken over; they insisted on being able to write responses to what people were doing and the company accommodated them. So you can twitter (or tweet) to an audience who are known to you, but you're just as likely to hook up with a complete stranger (but someone with whom you share a lot in common professionally or in terms of interests) as with someone you already talk to regularly. It's become a huge worldwide conversation and there are even people who think it's a better search engine than Google (it's probably not, and we'll look at why this is later on). Likewise, if I'd been writing about Facebook initially I'd have been talking about something for graduates only. It's now for anyone who wants to sign up but, unlike Twitter, it tries to insist you connect with people you actually know. I mean *really* know, people you've met.

The networks themselves change in their relative importance over time as well. A few years ago we'd have been talking about FriendsReunited a lot more than we will be in this book (it's just been put up for sale by ITV, which bought it from its founders a few years back; who knows, in a future edition we may yet be talking about it as a major player again). It's only a guess, but by the time this book sees publication I'd be very surprised if some of the initial Twittermania hadn't subsided. The history of social media and who's up and who's down is a fascinating subject, like the interplay between the players in any emerging industry. We'll be touching on it as a subject, but this book isn't intended as a comprehensive history of who's done what.

Instead, the book is aimed at business owners. Its main purpose is to offer a practical guide on how to use social media as part of your business. It looks at the networks and the technology of course, it would be nonsensical to attempt this sort of book without addressing those issues, but unlike some of the books on the market it looks directly at where these elements should fit into a good business plan. It won't assume you know how each connection is made with each social networking website, and it won't assume you're particularly interested in the technical jiggery-pokery that makes high-definition video recording so affordable and easy, nor how the data is compressed to get it onto YouTube without it taking a week to load. I'm going to assume you're just not interested in that stuff and that you'd prefer for me to:

● Get you familiar with YouTube and how to upload a video (and embed it onto your own site).

● Demystify Facebook and get you comfortable with setting up a profile and what to put on it.

● Ditto MySpace, Twitter and the rest.

● Assessing which, if any, of these networks are going to do your business any good and how you might measure the return on the time you'll be investing.

Before we get into that, though, it's worth having a look at how social networking actually arose, and why it's a very old idea indeed.

A brief background to social networking

I keep reading about how wonderfully thrilling and *new* the social networking area is. It's opened up the Internet to everyone, made the highest-flown celebrity available for a quick chat as long as you're not an obvious timewaster or aggressive, and it brings with it all sorts of new business rules and metrics.

But in fact I've been using this stuff since 1993 when I went freelance, and I have colleagues who've been using it in one form or another since the late 1980s. And it's very important to understand also that there are no new rules.

I've given talks about social networking to a number of organizations and I always get asked one or two questions about how you work with employees in this strange new environment. My answer is always the same: it isn't strange, it isn't new, it's the same employees as before working in the same environment. They just have a few new tools. In Chapter 1 we'll look at some specific examples of people who've assumed there is some new magic going on and that all the business sense you had before no longer applies, but for the moment I'd like to consider what happened around the turn of the century: the dotcom boom.

That was the last time people assumed there was some sort of new business paradigm. The exact moment I realized this was a huge mistake was when Time Warner bought Internet company AOL; the financial analysts suddenly had to revalue AOL (at a lower figure) because it had stepped into 'real' business and therefore needed to adhere to standard business rules rather than those that had evolved for dot-coms. Although the merger went ahead, inevitably many other dot-coms crashed as the commercial reality set in. It's the same this time around: social media need to be part of, not separate from, the commercial realities on which your business is based.

OK, so why do I say people have been using social networks since the late 1980s? In 1989 I started my first job as a trainee journalist on a computer publication in the UK, called *MicroScope*. Pedants will be aware that the Internet and in particular the technologies on which the World Wide Web was based were already around in primitive form, but for our purposes, even in a computer magazine, there was basically no such thing as an Internet just yet. We received copy from our contributors by post on floppy disks and our computers weren't even networked internally, we passed disks around. The system wasn't yet based on Windows and any thought of databases was best left to the experts.

By this stage any younger readers will be in tears at the deprivation we all suffered, but the reason I paint this picture is because of something one of the staff was doing in the corner. He was the quiet one and he had a job title that seemed to me a bit made up. But occasionally, someone would ask him a question and he'd come up with the answer a bit later without leaving his desk. I didn't understand how but he explained, when he felt like it, that he was 'On Kicks'. I later found out that he was actually accessing a system called Cix – Compulink Information eXchange – from his computer, logging in through the phone line.

Cix was – and is, you can still find it at www.cixonline.co.uk – a network of like-minded people, primarily technology types because they were the only people who knew how to work a modem (a gadget that predated broadband, for any *really* young readers) who'd log on for chat and information. (Beginning to sound familiar?)

It was text only, no pretty pictures, and it was divided up into 'conferences' (remember this is before Internet forums or anything like that) in various subject areas. There was 'Hacks' for journalists and more computing conferences than you'd really want to know about. It was into these conferences that my colleague would post his questions. If this sounds like a less random version of Twitter, then that's because the principle is similar.

I signed up for Cix when I went freelance in 1993. I discovered that you could use it to send files to people so I could work right up to the deadline. Then I found that you could also send to people who were not on Cix. That's because it was operating not only its own conferencing system but an Internet Service Provider business, very new stuff at the time. Cix was a really useful package and it even had its own front end, which allowed me to log on, download a load of messages and log off, which was useful before broadband to avoid clogging up the phone line.

However, the idea of a more visually interesting environment was taking root as computing was becoming more sophisticated and affordable. In the early 1990s company called CompuServe arrived in the UK. To the small number of us who used Cix the principle looked very similar; you dialled into the site and it put you through to lots of conferences – or forums, as they were called in CompuServe-ese. There were also a load of news services that were equally helpful, and the whole thing was laid out in a more visually appealing manner. If you were clever you could get a reader to take the messages off CompuServe and free up your phone line while you read them, much like you could with Cix. And the idea of joining an interest group online, being part of a community and being able to ask questions or get paid work from other journalists (or find a good supplier for your IT kit: I still use the computer seller I found on Cix many years ago and he's never let me down, email him on biz@cix.co.uk and he'll find whatever you're looking for) was the same.

CompuServe also had a gateway into something called the World Wide Web. I took a look once and didn't like it much, it was a bit of a free-for-all and you'd get a load of these 'website' things that basically said: 'Hi, I'm Larry and this is my dog.'

This started to change very slightly in 1995 with the emergence of America Online, now called simply AOL. Initially the company had the idea of putting together its own news content, and indeed in 1996 it hired me for a couple of years to put its technology news feed together and write an analysis piece every week (territorial claim no. 1: this must make me one of the first journalists in the UK paid to write specifically for online media). AOL also had forums for people in certain interest groups; technology types and a load of Star Trek fans. You could, again, do the social network thing in AOL's closed network. But before too long it became apparent that the real interest was in getting people onto the Internet.

There were other developments, like Internet forums and newsgroups, but everything became more sophisticated and easier when broadband arrived in the early 2000s. There was no financial penalty involved if you stayed online for ages, unlike in the old dial-up days, so taking part in an online forum no longer cost the earth or blocked your phone line.

It's against this backdrop that you can observe FriendsReunited, Facebook, Bebo, MySpace, Twitter and all the others coming into their own. The idea that they're desperately new, though, is plain misguided. The idea of social networking wasn't new, what had changed was the phenomenal ease of doing it and of course the numbers of people involved were growing exponentially. Now everything's gone very Web 2.0.

Web 2.0: My pet hate

You'll have heard a lot of people talking about Web 2.0. It's a way of describing the way the Internet is at the moment. Personally I hate the term: it suggests there's been a whole new version of the web (which is nonsense) and that there's a Web 3.0 on the way (I'm not aware of anyone planning one, but we can speculate on when the marketeers will start using that term).

What the proponents of Web 2.0 claim is that it signifies people starting to take part in what happened on the Internet, rather than absorbing it passively. When the Internet began being used widely in the 1990s, most businesses that had catalogues put them online, but your engagement was limited to putting your credit card details in. This started to change a little around the end of the last century (one day I'm going to feel really old writing sentences like that). People like Amazon let people put reviews of books and DVDs onto its site (quite brilliantly, it discovered reviewers would do this for no money), as did a few other sites, and then blogs emerged.

A blog, or web log, is more or less an online diary. The idea was that people would announce things that were interesting to them, share links to other interesting bits on the web and hopefully, although not necessarily, invite comments from other people. This is where Web 2.0 originated as far as I can see, when people started being part of the action. The debate about the 'democratization' of media also escalated as blogs expanded: what is the value of 'proper' journalists if so-called citizen journalists, or bloggers, are offering equal coverage?

The emergence of Facebook, Twitter and other social media applications amplified this effect. In December 2005 there was an explosion in Buncefield, UK. Many of the photographs in the press came from 'citizen snappers': people taking their own photos and sending them to the news agencies or increasingly putting them on photo sharing websites. As a more sinister example, in late 2008 there was a bomb in Mumbai and people reported what was happening through their Twitter accounts. The authorities asked them to stop because they were telling anyone who cared to log on exactly where the soldiers were going and where they were about to attack, risking giving the terrorists advance notice of where the city was most vulnerable.

My guess is that we'll be saying we're in Web 3.0 when we can all receive video and TV on demand through the Internet in super-high definition or 3D (I've seen it demonstrated and it's pretty impressive). That's a fair way off now and I really wouldn't worry about it: there may or may not be ways of taking advantage of that later.

What matters to a business owner is that when someone offers to make your website very Web 2.0, you need to know that they might not do much except put a blog on it (and this is a blog you'll be expected to write frequently, or else it's going to start looking very underused very quickly). Just as you need to be aware of what a mechanic's going to do to your car and why an oil change isn't worth thousands, you also need to know what some of the terms we'll be discussing mean and, above all, what you can expect from someone who wants to build your business around them.

So what's a social network?

A social network is an Internet-based tool that allows the reader to engage with the writer or with a community online and in public.

People seem to mean different things when they talk about social networks. Just so we're sure we all know what we're talking about, my definition appears on the left.

So your existing website probably isn't socially networked; Twitter and the rest are. A blog that allows comments is something we'll certainly look at; Wikipedia we'll mention because it's useful and has its pitfalls; whereas introducing your own wiki for your organization, in which you and a load of writers can add to the various definitions of terms and build up your own knowledge bank, is not public enough to be useful to enough readers for us to look at in a book like this. Basically, if you have specialist requirements, you need to talk to a specialist. This book will be about the stuff that's easy to get at and use.

Not just technology

Before we plunge into Chapter 1 I need to make one thing clear: this is a book about social networking technology as it can be applied to a business. You knew that. But it's important to stress that a lot of what social networking and Web 2.0 can achieve is also possible without using the Internet at all. The results and the scale will be different, but customer feedback has a long history.

For example, a lot of television programmes invite people to text comments in, and they have a blog or forum on which viewers can make comments. You may think this is new, but the BBC in the UK has run a programme called *Points of View* for decades, which invites viewers to write in – on paper, although now also email – and make their points, which get read out. Clearly, the programme allows for a lot less feedback than you'd get from an Internet forum, but it's there, nonetheless.

Likewise, the opportunity to comment on current affairs and news stories and join in a big conversation has been around for decades on both sides of the Atlantic in the form of radio phone-ins and letters pages in newspapers and magazines. The fact that now more people can participate because they have a medium that facilitates their inclusion rather than an editor cherry-picking something that fits the space doesn't make it revolutionary or new.

Think about your own customers. They interact with you somehow. If you run a restaurant their first point of contact is eating there; if they have a good experience they say so and come back, if they have a bad experience and they're British they say it's fine and just don't turn up again (American restaurant owners probably get a more honest response). If you're in a service industry you have feedback in different ways. Customers might recommend you, which is feedback; or you may hear some scuttlebutt about how your PA has halitosis if they don't like you, which is also feedback.

You might engage with customers and the public in all sorts of different ways. One company I spoke to before all this social media stuff happened made a point of paying for the cleaning of its local train station. This served two purposes: the community felt engaged by this organization brightening the place up, and any visitors came to a better-looking place to conduct their business.

The point I'm making is that although this book focuses on engaging with customers or indeed colleagues through electronic means, this needs to be part of your mix and not all you do. You run a garden centre and think your customers would respond better to a coffee morning than a blog? Great – spend your money that way. You run a consultancy and don't actually want to be perceived as having enough time to write a blog? Great, good reason, don't do it. But *do* find out what your customers are going to respond to, every time: don't just guess.

That's enough background. If you take anything away from this introduction, I hope it'll be something like:

- This isn't a magic bullet for my business.

- Using social networking, as long as it's appropriate, is an extension of what I'm already doing rather than something radical (so I don't have to be afraid of it!).

- I need to build this into my business plan and know why I'm doing it: which is what Chapter 1 is about.

THIS IS SOCIAL MEDIA

1 ONE SIZE WON'T FIT ALL

I'll start by saying something contentious: you might not need social media at all. This book doesn't advocate social media for the sake of it. Rather, it helps you look at your business and your desired outcome and work backwards to find the best way to achieve that. It's all about business planning and using the technology that's available and easy; it's not about how clever the technology itself is.

To be a little more constructive, social media may not be the answer to your business problem because there's every possibility you haven't defined the problem itself well enough yet. Throughout this book you'll find me looking for an objective, a desired outcome in any social media endeavour – this is a business book rather than something about leisure so you need to focus on that outcome.

Say you're a window cleaner in Edinburgh and you want more customers. You do a little decorating on the side and you'd like to make some more money out of this, so you set up a website and start writing a blog. I'm basing this on a real-life example of someone who once asked me how they could use the web to expand their window cleaning business.

So you've got the website and you've got the blog. We'll go into ways of putting a professional-looking blog up later, but for the moment let's assume it looks snazzy and you're not finding any technical problems. Now, what are you going to write on this new online diary? Let's guess:

- Monday, cleaned some windows.

- Tuesday, cleaned some windows.

- Wednesday, strained ankle slightly cleaning windows…

Apologies to any window cleaner reading this, you're probably an interesting person, but we're talking about a professional blog rather

A blog, or web log, is essentially an online diary you upload regularly to the Internet. Other people can subscribe and get your updates through a mail newsreader or other means, and they can also comment if you allow that.

than a personal one. Oh, and someone in Boulder. Colorado might think you sound like a really neat person to employ, but if you're in Edinburgh you're not going to decamp to America to clean this person's windows.

You don't need social media at all. What you need is to change the sign on your van to 'decorator' so people see it in the area in which you work. You need to change your written bills to include the word 'decorator' somewhere so that your existing customers, who already use your services quite happily, will think of you in another context. You can, if you're feeling flush, take out an ad in the local paper, or maybe – just maybe – an online directory like Yell.com. But you don't need social media.

As I've already said, this book won't bang on about technology for its own sake. For example, for a while I had my Facebook, Plaxo and Twitter feeds synchronized so that the updates always say the same thing, give or take a few minutes' updating across the different networks (don't worry about the names, we'll come on to those later). And I have no idea how it worked. I don't *want* to know how it works, just as I don't want to know exactly how my car works as long as it gets me around. What I care about is that once I was running about trying to keep a whole load of information feeds updated and now I don't have to. In other words, I knew which question I needed the technology to answer before I started adding bits to the way my set-up worked. That's the way we're going to work through this book – starting with an objective and working from there.

Your objective

Why did you buy (or borrow) this book? What was your objective? That's a serious question. It's not a book you'd buy for your leisure time or to unwind at the end of a long day. Presumably you bought it because you wanted to improve your existing business, or to start the right way when you begin a new one. One thing is almost certain though. When you bought the book you thought about your desired result and not the process. You didn't think: I'm going to walk into the store and lift this book off the shelf then take it to the checkout people and pay for it, or I'm going to buy it from an online bookseller. The process itself would have been of very little interest.

For some reason a lot of people lose sight of this when it comes to setting up some sort of social media for their business. They think: I ought to get onto Facebook because I've heard a lot of businesses are doing it; some people have apparently done well from appearing on MySpace, so I ought to do the same; I ought to be on Twitter because so is everybody else. So they focus on Facebook or MySpace rather than any likely outcome or what's going to go into making their use of these media effective. In no other part of their business will they have been so inclined to put a process in place as an end in itself. This book takes that idea apart and puts the desired outcome first.

So, what exactly do you want to achieve for your business through this strange new technology?

Let's say you want more customers; as straightforward as that. That's a respectable aim. Who exactly are your existing customers? How do they behave?

Start by thinking about how you regard certain categories of client. Get away from preconceptions and prejudgements. If you're selling to an older customer base, do you think they won't be using this stuff very much? When she heard I was writing this book, my mother-in-law told me she thought that was strange, as she didn't think I used

Facebook very much. *She* certainly did, to keep networked with her colleagues at the retail chain where she works. She'd been looking at my page and didn't think I was using it as well as I could. I now know my mother-in-law is monitoring my Facebook account: beware, it could be you!

She was mistaken in one thing: my use of Facebook is entirely appropriate for someone wanting to use it primarily as a source of sales leads and keeping in contact with editors. But I'd made the classic mistake of thinking someone from an older generation would be on other websites. If I'd been selling services or goods to my mother-in-law I'd have missed a possible means of contacting her, and a very cheap one at that.

So, who are your customers and how do they behave? Above all, do they behave as you think they do? There are ways of finding out. If you were going to take out an advertisement in a local newspaper, you'd find out which one your clients read by talking to them and asking. There's nothing wrong with getting a few customers to fill out a questionnaire and finding out what they actually do in terms of ordinary media, social media, how well they respond to fliers through the door, all that stuff.

Once you've found out a bit about if and how they use social media, read through the sections in Chapter 3 and think about what sort of expectations people on that network will have. It is simply no use sailing onto Twitter and announcing that you have a sale of cheap yachts happening from Saturday to Monday; only people who follow you voluntarily will find out about it. Here are a couple of basic guidelines that apply to most social media:

● Facebook, Twitter et al. have millions of users, but you won't be heard by all of them, people need to make a conscious decision to

follow you first. So in terms of attracting new customers a particular site might or might not be right; if someone's searching Twitter for your particular goods or service you might strike it lucky, but equally you might not.

- It's the same with setting up a profile on Facebook, or even a discussion group or forum. Never forget that you'll be seen only by your 'friends', people who've decided to hook up with you on the site. It's a bit like the early days of the Internet when some people thought just putting a website up would increase their business, and were then bewildered when it didn't do so. People have to be persuaded to come to your website or your Facebook page. Then you have to keep them there with compelling information, competitions, whatever is appropriate. Fail to attract the customer and you might as well be knocking at the door of an empty house trying to sell your wares.

I'm not trying to put you off, it's just a matter of working from the desired outcome backwards. Let's continue assuming that you want new customers; say, 10 more people to come into your classical music shop. Working backwards, how do these people get into your shop? How do they hear about it?

Crucially, do they *all* hear about it through social media? I'll bet they don't. If you're going to get to all your potential customers, then working backwards should help you get an idea of what you need: word of mouth, local ads, and yes, probably social networks. Remember the word 'networks', it's particularly important. A network is an engaged group of people who've spoken to each other and told their friends about you. So, working backwards another step, what did they tell each other? Presumably not that you go online every five minutes to advertise your shop. They might, though, tell each other if you were a particularly knowledgeable source of information on

classical music; maybe you have a particular passion for Baroque and can answer just about any question that's put to you in that area. That's something that might well get classical music buffs flooding to your Facebook site in numbers. At that point you might want to think about whether you should sell online too if you have enough customers, so you link your Facebook site to an online store and people start buying from you after engaging with you for some advice. You might find the profile of your customers has changed a little, but that doesn't matter. In this instance you've found a new set of customers and it didn't cost much. You've learned that engagement comes before the exchange of money and that's also fine. It's a productive use of your time.

Getting new customers is one objective, making more money out of your existing customers is another. New customers are and difficult to find, while making more money out of your existing customers is frequently easier and cheaper, as you're likely to get their attention a great deal more easily. The question is how to make them spend more or somehow become an advocate of your brand, which you can often achieve through social media.

In the preface we looked at photographer Simon Apps and his success using Twitter. It's interesting to note that his objective was pretty clearly to attract more customers, but to do this he had to get away from simply being corporate. 'I found trying to do corporate tweets that were suitable to appear on the website very difficult and to be honest, quite boring. So within a week I had created a new Twitter account, @simonapps, which is not published on the front page of the site but deeper within the site on my biog page at http://www.professional-images.com/who.htm, therefore making it clear that it was my personal account,' he says. 'It is this account that has attracted the followers, so I guess I must be doing something right! Clearly, building a relationship

Unfollowed means dropped from another Tweeter's radar. If you've been unfollowed they won't see your tweets any more.

with the person and not the business is the way to go. Personally I find people I follow that do nothing but try and sell their services extremely tedious and tend to ignore them whilst scanning through the tweets of those I'm following. Ultimately they will be unfollowed.'

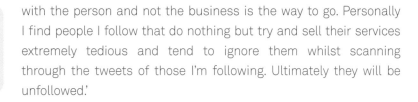

Rose and Crown

Rose and Crown is a hairdresser in London's Covent Garden area. It's trendy and up market, but it's in a basement and not easy to find unless you're looking for it. It's competing with the likes of Trevor Sorbie and Nicky Clarke, the actual salons in which the famous hairdressers work rather than a franchise of some sort. The owner felt that word of mouth would be the best way to get people through the door, so he registered with a local online directory (we'll come to those in Chapter 4). This directory allowed people to add reviews of where they'd been, such as hairdressers and restaurants. The owner wasn't concerned about bad reviews, because everybody gets those from time to time, but he wanted to increase his visibility. Reviews started coming in and so did more customers. Rather cleverly, he now has a laptop in his foyer so if anyone feels like reviewing their experience quickly before they leave, they can do so. This means Rose and Crown actually gets more reviews than everyone else because it's convenient for customers to leave a note on the site. The few negative reviews actually add some credibility.

Larger organizations have found that encouraging their customers to participate somehow is a good way of getting them to engage with other potential customers. For example, Spinvox is a service that converts voicemails into text so that they can be picked up regardless of background noise. The company revamped its website to coincide with a trade show at which it was exhibiting. Many of its customers went onto their Twitter accounts and started a debate about just how much they disliked the new look and feel of the site. Spinvox's communications manager James Whatley was also on Twitter, though, and he was able to respond; making it clear that he wasn't there to apologize for not meeting an individual's likes or dislikes, but stressing that his company was listening. He was able to respond to some of the concerns and the coverage turned slowly from bile to more settled messages.

'Also, it's worth noting that on the day of hostile feedback I made sure I replied to *every single* criticism with a fair and reasonable response. We let the community at large know we were listening and every single tweet was seen by the senior development team,' says Whatley. 'Great stuff that continues to influence our decision-making process to this day.'

Likewise, there was an occasion on which ITV was covering an FA Cup football match and was unlucky enough to cut to the adverts when the only goal was scored. Twitter went crazy with fans saying what rubbish ITV was. The company's communities assistant Gary Andrews, who is also on Twitter, was able to engage with the complainers, assured them he shared their frustration at not seeing the goal and promised to find out what went wrong. There was no getting away from the fact that someone had goofed, and in a big way, but the contempt subsided quite quickly. ITV was seen to be listening.

'I immediately got several texts from friends asking me what was going on. As soon as I'd established what had been broadcast, I logged onto Twitter on my personal account and posted a couple of messages along the lines of I couldn't say what had happened as I didn't know myself, but would be doing my best to find out in the morning and posting as much on Twitter about the incident as I was able to say and told them to check the ITV feed. I then went onto ITV's official account, apologized, again stressed we couldn't say why it had happened but as soon as we knew, we would post links and information,' says Andrews. Things changed quickly: 'Up to that point most of my Twitter stream had been filled with very angry comments about the game. Once I'd posted, people were actually a lot kinder (probably realizing that I'd be having to deal with the firefighting the next morning). There was a bit of gentle ribbing, plenty of 'thank yous' for at least coming onto Twitter and saying something and once the Tweets had been passed around, it seemed, on my stream at least, people had calmed down.'

Stream: in Twitter terms your 'stream' means all of the messages that reach you.

Did the companies in the last two examples get extra sales or customers out of these engagements? I doubt it. Did they want to? I doubt that too. They were both using their chosen social media – and they could have achieved much the same on Facebook – to sustain contact and take part in a conversation with their existing customers or viewers. They had their objective, they had ascertained that their customers would be on Twitter and they used that medium to achieve their desired outcome.

Here's a flow chart of how a lot of people work out their social media strategy:

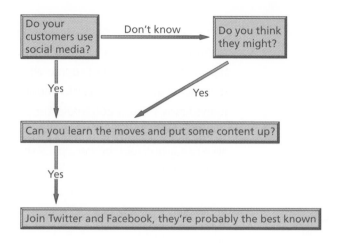

Here's a flow chart about how you ought to be doing it:

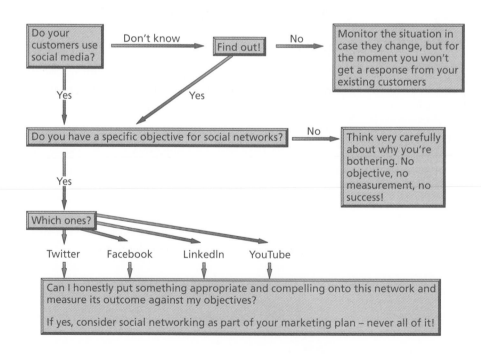

You'll notice something specific about my 'better way': it puts the customer first, then a specific objective. Here's an important point: this is in no way unique. It is how the best business plans work: they look at the desired outcome and how best to get there, and they follow the plan. Granted that external factors, like the economy, can work against you, but overall your business plan should be there to serve a purpose rather than to serve the business in its own right.

Budgeting your social media activities

As a business owner you need to look at social media not just as an add-on to your marketing, bolted on as some sort of afterthought; you need to look at social media as a central part of your company and something that matters a great deal to you. It needs to be in your business plan and it needs to be thought through. Questions to ask yourself include:

- What am I aiming to achieve through social media?

- Is this realistic?

- Is it budgeted?

- Is it measurable?

- Can it turn around and bite me later on?

You can then start putting this into your business plan. Don't skip this step – if it's going to be any use, social networking needs to be part of your overall strategy.

And it *needs* to be budgeted. You may think that social networking is mostly free, and up to a point it is. Much of it – the blogging space, Twitter and Facebook membership – won't cost a penny.

But let's have a look at where money does start to become an issue:

- **Free stuff:** blogging space (basic, although of course you can spend money on web space too), Twitter/Facebook/LinkedIn/ Plaxo/other network membership.

- **Name:** fancy a catchier name for your blog? When I set up the blog to go with this book at http://guyclapperton.wordpress.com, I soon realized that this wouldn't be a catchy title, so I spent £8.99 on the domain www.socialnetworkingblog.co.uk for two years.

- **Content:** let's continue to use my blog as an example. I write for a living and I wanted a good blog with some depth (and a load of established entries) to help promote the book – in other words, I had a reason to write it for no money up front, but it's time I would otherwise be spending earning cash. You'll either have to do the same or ask a member of staff to do it. Staff members given extra duties are inclined to want extra payment or extra incentives of some sort and all of this will take up resources. You might find you want to outsource the writing to a professional; that costs, too.

- **Monitoring:** if you want someone to monitor Twitter or Facebook for mentions of your company and address any difficult people posting about you, you'll have to build it into an existing person's job or hire someone new. As this book was being commissioned I saw that Sky News had advertised to hire someone specifically to monitor Twitter. Unless you're a news gathering agency yourself you're unlikely to have to do that, but all of this stuff is going to take time. And time costs money.

- **Marketing:** you want a newsletter to keep your customers informed of your new offers and services? Great, but you'll need to pay an editor, a writer and a designer and if you want a physical newsletter then there will be printing and delivery costs. Don't write the idea off: it might be exactly right for your customers and only you're going to know that. But putting bulletins up on Facebook or adding a video interview to YouTube instead of relying on plain text to get attention can get to as many people if you market it properly and will cost a great deal less. Maybe you want to do some cold calling? That's equally time consuming and most people say 'no thanks'. Let's say you sell or service vintage cars and you want to get more customers. You can probably source a list of owners to cold call, but some of them will no longer own their vehicles, a percentage will have died, and the list could all be out of date depending on its age. You might get better results by looking for blogs on the subject and trying to engage with the writers; a well-read and well-regarded blog giving you a positive mention is likely to attract a lot more attention than a cold call from someone the recipient doesn't know.

- **Legal:** if you want, sensibly, to put together an acceptable use policy of some description for your social media (we'll come to this in Chapter 6), you'll need to factor in some sort of payment for your solicitor.

The activity's not a pushover then, but there are a load of benefits to be had from good, competent use of social media. Take the hairdresser we were discussing earlier. Take Spinvox and ITV talking their customers down when they were becoming belligerent and turning some of them into advocates for the brand they'd only just been trashing. Take media companies, an obvious area for social networks and one in which Channel 4 News has managed to engage with its viewers and so has the BBC's *Working Lunch*, to the point of reading some of its viewers' tweets on the air and indeed sourcing interviewees with expertise in particular areas.

It's not just media companies either. The London Club organizes events in the evening and boosts its numbers by making sure social networking is part of its marketing mix, having first looked at the profile of its customers and where they're likely to be. As another example, a small business investor went on Twitter to allow people to contact him but also – and this is the really clever bit – to force them to distil their proposals into a really short message, which saves him time and means they have to really, really think about what they're writing.

There are plenty more. There's a trainer and life coach who gives a free one-hour session over Twitter once a week and finds he gets loads of new customers moving on to the paid-for services afterwards. The Arctic Monkeys didn't put their own songs on MySpace, that was the fans, but doing so shot them into the charts and international success. I grant you, you're probably not going to be a star like the Arctic Monkeys, but entertainment is another business that social networking has pushed forward. It's done brilliantly and there's no reason you shouldn't do as well by the same low-cost means.

If you take only one thing away from this chapter it will ideally be that your use of social media in your business needs to be strategic and planned rather than haphazard.

Action points

At the end of every chapter I'll be putting in some action points, something you can actually go away and do. The doesn't make this some sort of 'in 24 hours' guide; for example some of today's points will take longer than some of the suggestions in the rest of the book. But here are two sets of actions. One is stuff to think about – *really* think about it or you've wasted your money on this book – and the other is on stuff to go and do.

Thinking matter

1. Who are your customers and where do they get their information on your services?

2. How old are your customers; are they likely to engage with social media already, and if not will they do so in future? Filling in the table here might help crystallize this in your mind. Use whichever age group or other variant you want.

3. Is there someone out there who is already posing as your business (yes, this does happen)? Or worse, is there an authentic employee out there who people think represents 'your voice'? We'll come on to examples where this has actually happened in Chapter 6.

Customer age group	Social network members (yes or no)	Which social networks	Named member of staff who can address this network	Probable cost in time	Probable increased income as a result	Increased profit?
18–30						
30–55						
55+						

Do list

- Start to redraft your business plan and incorporate social media in it if you're convinced that's appropriate.

- Set specific targets: if you want to bring more people to your website through social media, decide how many and keep reality checking it. Measure your success.

- Move on to Chapter 2 – we're not ready to set a revised business plan in stone just yet!

2 YOUR BUSINESS AS THE RECIPIENT OF SOCIAL MEDIA

In Chapter 3 we'll look at the mechanics of getting yourself onto the social media site or sites (or networks, some of them aren't really sites) of your choice. In fact we'll have a look at how to choose the social network of your choice. If you can't wait, feel free to skip ahead. Only I wouldn't.

This is the chapter in which you step back and learn a bit from observing the networking sites before you leap in. You might find a lot out about your own company and its readiness to engage in social media in the process.

Vanity Googling

Google: one of the most popular search engines on the Internet as we went to press, see www. google.co.uk or www. google.com.

Have you ever heard the phrase Vanity Googling? Also called self-Googling and a number of other less than complimentary names, it consists of searching for yourself and your company on Google, or the search engine of your choice (many of which are Google in disguise).

But, you scoff, what sort of oaf is going search for themselves? You're the expert in your own business, you know what's going on better than anyone else. What is this, an exercise in vanity?

Well, yes and no. Let me tell you what happened to a friend of a colleague (it wasn't me, it was really that distant). He ran a small business, conceivably just like many people reading this book. He employed a number of people and one day one of them, a young woman, came into his office and said she was taking him to a tribunal for harassing her sexually. I stress that he had done no such thing.

He was understandably aghast. She insisted she was taking him to court because he'd said she looked like the sort of girl who liked to take it up the **** (I'm not going to finish that sentence in a business book) and she was suing him. She told the local press. They ran a story.

He was bewildered and shaken – until he did some digging around and found out that she'd done the same thing to three previous employers, each of whom had given her £4,000 in an out-of-court settlement rather than be dragged through the tribunal process. He confronted her with this and she backed down immediately. He told the local press, they ran another story, honour was satisfied.

So why am I telling you this? The answer is quite simple. The manager in question realized immediately that anyone who was doing a search on him or his company would be just as likely to come across the initial allegation as the outcome in which he was exonerated. Understanding this, he carried a sheaf of photocopies of the exoneration story with him so that if a journalist asked about the allegation he could prove beyond doubt that he was innocent.

A false allegation that gets repeated in the press gets into the search engines and could get under your skin if you're the wronged individual or company; you'll only know about it if you do a 'vanity Google' on yourself and your business once in a while.

Vanity Twittering, Facebooking, MySpacing...

The bad news is that it doesn't stop with websites, although Google is a pretty good way of finding other things too. There are three main problems you're looking for when you look for yourself in social media.

The first is imposters. This is something that happens to celebrities more than to most small businesses (although let's not forget that most of these celebs are themselves self-employed sole trading businesses). I'll give you an example. In early 2009, the UK's biennial charity event Comic Relief had a competition for celebrities recreating classic dance routines from the movies. Comedian Robert Webb recreated Flashdance, complete with wig and leotard, and made a huge wad of cash for the charity in the process. So far, so excellent (and you can still catch the clip on YouTube). People congratulated Webb on his Twitter account, it was a great way of getting in touch in a non-intrusive way...but it wasn't him. Realrobertwebb set up his own account to alert people that they were actually talking to a fake.

Other examples abound: there have been fake Jeremy Clarksons and Britney Spears, and loads of others. The vast majority are just people having a laugh; they *can* be mistaken for the real person so they have a go, to entertain themselves. Others have different reasons – after the European elections of 2009 someone set up 'Realnickgriffin' on Twitter, named after the leader of the British National Party; his or her rants are hysterically funny.

The fakes can be entertaining but they could also do something damaging. The fake Britney – actually her real account, populated by a crack squad of public relations people and then either hacked or one of them took a dislike to the singer – announced at one stage that a certain element of her anatomy was 4ft wide and full of teeth. This was so ludicrous nobody would have mistaken it for the real Britney, so no damage was done other than a little embarrassment, but suppose 'Britney' had said something contemptuous of her fans? Suppose someone claiming to be a drinks manufacturer said they felt they were lucky to have passed through a recent environmental health swoop, or even hinted that there had been such a swoop?

You begin to see how this can backfire on you if it's not monitored and kept under control. You can of course do nothing about a faker if you can't find them, but you can certainly alert the owners of the network, whether it's Facebook, Twitter or whoever else, that someone is posing as your business with a view to damaging you. If you have reasonable evidence that this is indeed happening, there's every chance they'll help immediately.

Cybersquatting: taking someone else's name for your own use on the Internet.

Go back to basic business planning as well: is someone infringing your product name with the name they're using? If trademarking hasn't been in your plan, consider your position – the price of registering one came down in 2009, so have you done enough to protect your intellectual property?

We're back to the principle that there are no special rules for new media. It's just the old rules written again and applied to a different backdrop. Protection of your intellectual property and some regard for managing your brand comes into straightforward, ordinary business practice and planning.

Intellectual property: anything you own that is intangible – your trademarks, your trading name, your online identity.

The second category you need to look for is complainers. Once again, the difficulties and the rules are exactly the same when you're dealing with complaints in the old or the new world. You need to be responsive: immediately that phone rings and doesn't get answered quickly, you can have a problem; failing to reply to a letter – or if you're from certain companies replying in something you think is English but which actually doesn't even skirt the issue – is all too common. I know, I've written to the bank once or twice.

Complainers on public social networks can do a lot of damage, though. Again, you can find a lot of them by Googling your company, but watch also to see whether you're being blogged about. If there's someone who's known not to be in favour of your organization, try Googling them as well – they might be blogging about you under their own name. Right now.

The critic becomes the advocate

Mostly the complainers will be straightforward enough. Christopher Ward of London is a British watchmaker whose main office is now in Buckinghamshire (www.christopherward. co.uk). There's a story we'll come to later about how the organization came to have an independent forum dedicated to its website, but for the moment all you need to know is that it's there.

The forum members tend to be fans, they enjoy owning more than one watch and specifically they own more than one Christopher Ward watch. The maker released an update to one of its watch models and one of the forum members – calling himself The Terminator (forum members invariably include someone naming themselves after a movie character) – said it wasn't good enough. He liked it but it needed to be done in gold, with a black face… he continued for some time.

'So we thought we'd make it,' explained Christopher Ward himself. The company went about developing this watch. They made about 100 – any fewer and the economies of scale fail to kick in (it would need to be a much larger order except that it used a standard casing) – and called it the Terminator Limited Edition.

The Terminator himself ended up with a watch named after him from one of his favourite manufacturers, to his specification. He was over the proverbial moon. The forum went into overdrive ordering the limited edition and it's now an annual event: the forum members chip in with what they'd like to see Christopher Ward of London do with watch design and the company launches a limited edition.

The good thing about social networks is that they're increasingly searchable in their own right. For example, in Twitter people can use something called a 'hashtag' when they want to start a discussion about something specific. It looks like this: # followed by the subject they want to discuss. A search for #reddwarf or any other cult TV programme inevitably leads to loads of results from people who're using the network socially rather than for business or serious research. A search for #yourcompanyname will tell you whether there's anything being said about you, positive or negative, at any one time.

The hashtag is useful for people setting up a discussion in a premeditated manner; perhaps you're more likely to get a more casual mention, in which case leave the hashtag off and search for your name alone. Your only problem here is that if you have a Twitter account under your own name you'll find all of your own tweets and replies as well as people replying to you. Facebook and the others are likewise searchable and if you search for your company name on LinkedIn and save the search, it'll do it again once a week so you get constant updating.

One of the worst things about finding a complainer in a social network is that if you can see them, so can everyone else. There's no need to panic. The fact that Twitter had – as this chapter was being written – some six million members worldwide doesn't mean they're all looking at the entry on your company at any given time. We'll come on to how you can use Twitter in the next chapter, but for the moment all you need to know is that even if Barack Obama (a frequently followed Tweeter) were to say something nasty about your business (and he won't!), only 800,000 of them will see the message and a huge percentage of those will miss it among the mass of other messages they receive.

Nevertheless, if someone trashes your business and allows everyone to see it, you can respond to it and hopefully turn the situation around in an equally public way.

Carphone Warehouse

Carphone Warehouse has monitored Twitter and found examples of negative in-store customer groups. In one instance someone complained – on the Twitter network, not in the store – that a salesperson was trying to sell him phone plans as if they were dodgy watches. Carphone Warehouse sent an immediate tweet back, offering to help, and the customer started being more positive, at least thanking them for the approach.

The customer and the company began to send emails. The customer told the marketing rep exactly what had gone wrong and where, and although the company still lost the customer on this occasion, he said he'd consider going back next time he changed his phone; he also tweeted about his good engagement with the company and its positive approach.

On another occasion there had been an error with a cheque sent to a customer and the bank had refused to accept it. Once again, the Carphone Warehouse people saw the complaint on Twitter before they had a chance to receive a formal complaint. They asked for details informally on Twitter, took it to email and were able to resolve the complaint *and* get a positive message about their approach before it escalated. Better still, the customer involved was a blogger and blogged not about the initial issue (everyone accepts that mistakes happen) but the positive resolution.

Another customer posted a complaint on a website called ComplaintCommunity. This blog entry detailed how an offer hadn't been honoured; once again, by monitoring websites and responding to complaints being made online, the company was able not only to satisfy the customer but to receive a fulsome endorsement on the same site about how it had responded.

There are other cases as well, but this is a good illustration of how customer care can annex social media as part of a deliberate strategy.

And now some positives

You can find unexpected good news when you look, too.

It would be wrong to stress too much that you're looking for bad news when you're Googling and checking yourself out on social media for howlers, imposters, complainers and overzealous staff. You can also look for a load of positives before you've started posting anything yourself.

For example, you might find you have an unexpected advocate in the market. It happens; someone has had some really good customer service, so they write about it online. As we established in the previous chapter, this can be even better when you actually engage with them, but being aware that someone is posting positive stuff about you can work very much to your advantage.

Take the example of the aforementioned Christopher Ward watches (www.christopherward.co.uk). This independent watchmaker started attracting attention from the Timezone web discussion forum. Christopher Ward claimed it was offering quality watches, Swiss movements and those sorts of features for a lower than usual price. One of the members of the forum decided to buy one and take it apart to find what was really in the casing. He was pleasantly surprised and said so; to the extent that the owners of the forum assumed he was a plant from the company and asked him to pipe down. 'We knew nothing about it, in fact,' said Ward. 'But you could see how it looked.'

It was in fact at this stage that the watch company itself became aware that it had this advocate in the community. It allowed him some space on its own website and set up a forum to discuss Christopher Ward watches only. The result is a sort of informal owners' club. The members feel a sense of community as a result and they go out effectively as ambassadors for the brand.

Finding that you have positive press for which you hadn't accounted can tell you a lot about what people are looking for from your business; it can also nudge you in directions you hadn't considered. Limited edition watches to cater for a minority forum has opened up a whole new business area. If people are recommending you for a particular reason or suggesting your business has a particular strength, you may be able to build that into your marketing.

Customer care

Let's think for a moment about how customers contact you for customer care. Is there a way you could use social networking to improve the way you work this? Let's have a look at a diagram of how it might work at the moment:

Traditional customer care touch points

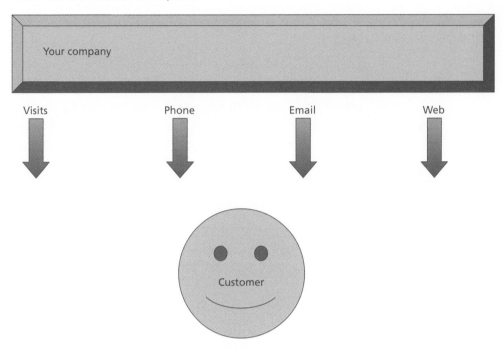

This is pretty basic stuff. Included on the diagram is the provision of some sort of self-service, let's assume a frequently asked questions section, or maybe you even have one of those questionnaire-style self-help widgets.

Now let's add social networks to the equation.

Customer care touch points with social networking built in

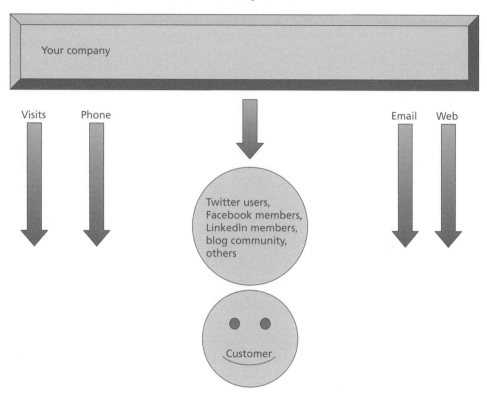

Notice a few things. First, you're not bypassing the customer: if you're wise, you won't use social networks or anything else as a barrier, you'll use them as an additional touch point. The customer can still get in touch with your business in exactly the same way he or she could before. He or she can also give you a prod through Facebook or LinkedIn, or wherever else you're active.

That's not what I wanted to illustrate through this diagram, though. Let's use a real example, one we've seen already in this chapter, Christopher Ward and his watchmaking business. If you buy components in currencies other than sterling, you may have seen your company suffer when the pound started to slip, as it did in early 2009. Christopher Ward was buying movements for its watches in Euros and the result was that they went up in price.

So far, so basic. But one or two of the forum members were less than amused. The company always offered quality for a good price, so they wanted to know what was going on. Before any of the staff could take action, one of the forum members responded with a comment about rising costs being passed on. So by using social networks, the company was able to get the customers to act as their own customer care network in the first instance.

Forum: an online discussion group people can join, with comments visible on the web.

Clearly, this doesn't work every time, but do yourself a favour: go and have a look at some of the technology support forums for when a computer goes down. Customers almost always ask a question online before they go back to the manufacturer for a definitive answer. Now, ask yourself how much money such a company is saving on support staff for basic customer support issues.

In fact, have you ever asked a computer-related question on an Internet forum and saved a company some money in customer care activities? Did you think any less of the company as a result? It could be that there is money waiting to be saved for you.

A link or 'hotlink' on a website is text that leads directly to another website or activates an email link, just by clicking on it.

Let people know

We'll come on to how you get people to find you online in Chapter 5, but it's worth pausing slightly to make sure you're telling people about your social networking activity. If you set up a forum, it needs to be plastered somewhere on the front page of your website; don't worry about putting it on your business card, people who don't go to the web won't care anyway. Your Twitter address, Facebook page and anything else you want to use as an alternative front page for your business need to be on your literature somewhere, too.

If you can't fit it all onto a business card – and believe me, once you have more than a couple of networks active you can't fit everything in – then you might want to look at something like a .tel listing (again, Chapter 5 will help you through this). Meanwhile, make sure there's a page on your website clearly labelled 'networks'; people who know what they're looking for will go straight there. There are software buttons available from all the social networks to put on these pages so that when someone clicks on them they're taken to the right page on the right network. Have a look at mine at www. clapperton.co.uk on the 'social networks' tab; you can find my links to Facebook, Plaxo, LinkedIn and other networking sites on that page.

If you can accommodate the links on the front page of your site, so much the better: people will see them immediately they go to your website.

Action points

Thinking matter

1. You might think you have no social media presence, but is someone else likely to have created one for you? Is there actually a similarly spelt company or any misconception about you that you could find or neutralize?

2. Do you have any employees who are likely to have put some social media content up on your behalf, officially or otherwise?

3. Are there ways in which your customers would be happy to help each other rather than rely on your paid staff when there's a problem? And would they mind this?

Do list

- If you didn't do it at the beginning of this chapter, Google your company immediately and see what you find.

- Try joining in a discussion that involves a Twitter hashtag to get the hang of them.

- Look at the space on your website and have a think about where buttons to let people know you're now in social media might go.

3 A WHO'S WHO OF SOCIAL MEDIA

Now you have some appreciation of the social media landscape, and before I get you started on a social media network, I need to establish who the key players are in some depth. You probably know Bebo is vaguely for young people and Facebook started as a business application, but by the end of this chapter, if you read it all the way through, you're going to be an expert in all of them.

This is not an exhaustive list. Wikipedia has a list of 150 social networks and you don't need them all. Even if you take the ones devoted to dating and teenagers out of it, and then arbitrarily exclude the non-English language models, you're still in three figures. I've therefore been selective. I'm listing nothing niche, and nothing that looks too unbusinesslike (so the extremely popular music services last.fm and Spotify don't qualify). English-language services that are more popular overseas I've also disallowed, so there's no Orkut in here (apologies to Indian and Brazilian readers, who probably love this Google-owned service). Services that have been huge but have been up for sale for months with no buyer are likewise excluded, with apologies to FriendsReunited (which was sold off as this book went to press but whose future plans have yet to be announced – I'm expecting some sort of relaunch).

You'll get more out of this chapter if you look at it for reference; look stuff up when you need it, not before. I'm going to be very strict with the format, too; name, what it is, audience, how to get involved, applications and add-ons, hints and tips.

So here we are, the main players in alphabetical order.

Bebo

One of the earliest of the current batch of social networking sites, Bebo was founded in 2005 and its name stands for 'Blog Early, Blog Often.' It marketed itself initially as an extension of college and high school, a tendency that increased when it was acquired by AOL. People with existing AOL accounts and Skype accounts can now add them to their Bebo log-ins. It's noted for being the place where the award-winning drama *KateModern* originated.

What is it?

If you're not into multimedia, video and music, do yourself a favour – forget Bebo right now. Bebo is one of the places on which people like to display their creative wares. It's creative, creative, creative. A company marketing videos or one marketing products that lend themselves to being demonstrated would do well on Bebo; a company selling cattle feed frankly wouldn't.

The question is whether Bebo's going to be superseded by YouTube at some point. The jury remains out on that one, although its main competitor has until now been MySpace.

Who uses it?

Although the majority of social networking participants in 2008 were over 35, Bebo remains true to its roots and has a large percentage of teenagers taking part. It's possibly among the most focused social media sites there is. It's pretty rigidly dedicated to leisure time as well; there's little room for serious content.

What's in it for a business?

A rigidly defined group of young users, one of the best defined on the Internet. As long as Bebo continues to grow, at least a little, this should be a gift to marketeers in the area.

How to get involved

First, make sure you have plenty of creative goodies to offer, whether that's music or video.

Second, go to www.bebo.co.uk and hit the button marked 'Sign up'.

Web browsers

Most PCs come with Internet Explorer as the default web browser, most Macs with Safari. It can be worth having a second browser installed for two reasons: if there's a software problem with the first you're not stuck, and websites can display differently on different browsers. Firefox (www.firefox.com) is an excellent alternative and works across all common hardware platforms; Flock (www.flock.com) is a tweak of Firefox that aims to accommodate social media better than most. Both are worth looking at. The pictures throughout this section were taken using Google's Chrome, another free download, on a Mac running Windows.

You're taken to a simple form: put your details in and fill in the box with the letters they're displaying to prove you're not an automatic spam machine. The next screen asks you to invite your friends to join your network. You've now joined and can start filling more details in.

The most important elements for you will be the picture box and the video box. Once you have a video on your computer, you can upload it immediately by using this box; click 'upload' and it'll ask where on your computer the file is. Find it, click 'upload' and it'll do just that. It's all very straightforward.

Applications and add-ons

Very few, but you can go into the menu on the top left-hand corner of your start page and get a button for your website that will take people straight to your homepage on Bebo.

Tips and tricks

- Be creative.

- Be ready to engage – this is not an audience that will respond well to a sales pitch, most of them are teenagers.

- Be patient. This isn't a natural place to do business. The market is there and you can establish a lot in terms of branding, but 'please buy my product' is going to get you abuse and not much else.

Blellow

Blellow was a very new service as this book went to print. It's American, as are most of them, and it has only a handful of UK customers. This may or may not change; it's impossible to tell at this stage.

Without wishing to belittle the efforts of the owners to do something different, you could usefully describe Blellow as a sort of Twitter lookalike for the business world. Rather than 'What Are You Doing Now?' its catchline is 'What Are You Working On?'

What is it?

Blellow looks and feels a lot like Twitter when you first sign up. The emphasis is on short text-only messages, accompanied by an optional mugshot. People mostly use genuine pictures rather than the more idiosyncratic 'personality' pictures favoured by those on more 'social' social networking sites.

Dig a little deeper and there's a lot more to Blellow, although given the newness of the service and the consequent minimal number of users there's more potential than actual stuff happening. You can, for example, set up a group – you can do this on Twitter as well, but it's not as clearly signalled for the first-time user from the home page. There is also a tab for starting a discussion about a specific project for which you're seeking help, or advertising a job, or setting up a meeting. There is also the inevitable blog about what's happening with the service; again, dig deeper and you'll find this in most of the services under discussion, but Blellow makes it a lot easier to find.

All Blellow lacks is a significant number of people, which wouldn't be fair to expect at this early stage. It has all the right ingredients in place to become a very useful place: the market will decide what happens.

Who uses it?

Blellow is determined that it's going to be a business meeting place and its structures and spaces for meetings and so on suggests it's going the right way about it. The design and opportunity to network with like-minded people indicate that it's going to be the smaller rather than the larger company that's going to take part; as a jobbing freelance I'd find it very useful if people put up work opportunities for me, for example, but a larger company is likely to look for an agency for one-off project work.

The people currently using the site have an informal view of their professional roles; they are there as people first, companies second. This is a pretty typical view of social networkers, but in Blellow's case they have an idea of why they're there rather than just 'having a look around'.

What's in it for a business?

Blellow represents an excellent networking and marketing opportunity for smaller businesses who don't know where else to go for help just yet, although not knowing where to go might be a symptom of a bigger business problem. Assuming it grows, it should be able to take the best elements of many of the other networks and apply them to the business world.

How to get involved

Joining Blellow is free and very simple indeed. The home page at www.blellow.com has a sign-up button.

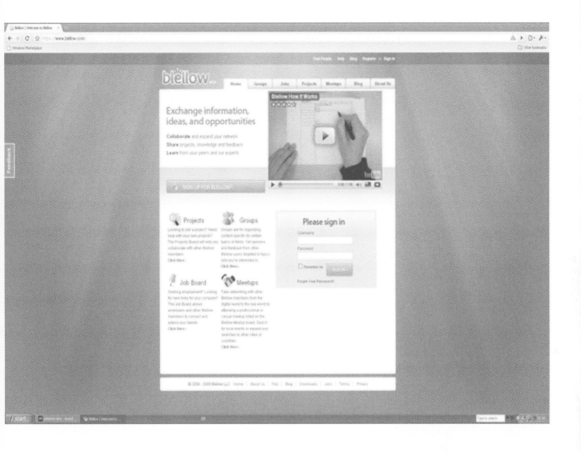

Click on it and choose a user name and password. You'll then be sent a link to click and activate your account. The next page you'll see offers to check your Twitter contacts, Gmail contacts and others to see whether you know anyone who's already on the service. Entering your passwords on this site appears to be safe.

After this or clicking the 'No thanks I'll do that later' button you reach the dashboard. At this stage, unless you've added people through Twitter, AOL or the other services as outlined above, you'll have a pretty dull screen in front of you telling you that you have 0 followers, 0 messages and basically no mates, because nobody knows you're there. You can add a photo by clicking on the photo icon, but we're going to click 'Create my profile'. You can see both of these below.

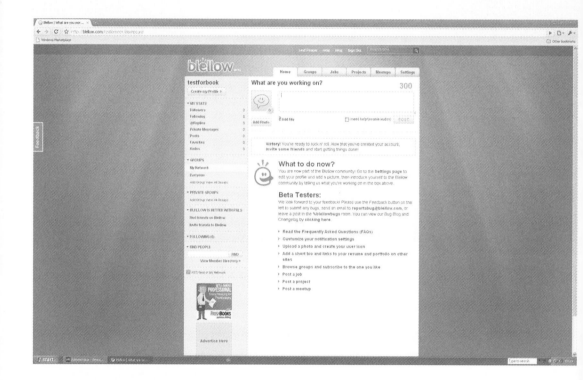

You'll be taken to the profile screen. Be brief: describing what you do is limited to 50 words and it's what people will see when they click through for more details.

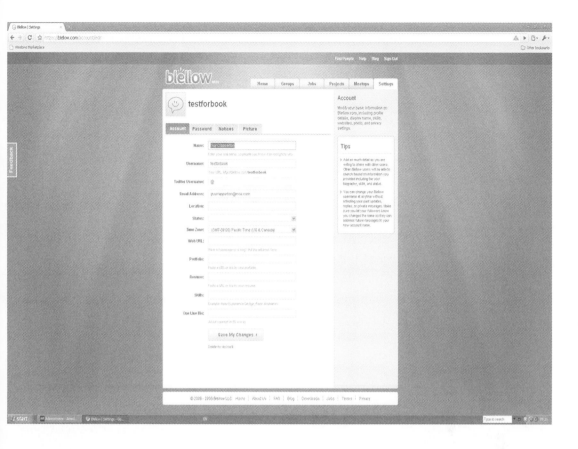

Hit 'Save' and your account settings will be updated automatically. Click back to the home tab and you can make your first entry and please, please don't just tell people you're joining Blellow, everyone does that on every social network for their first message. Have a look at the 'Group' section, see what's relevant to you in there and join a few; there's a UK group, which is small for the moment.

Applications and add-ons

Very few for the moment. At the time of writing you could download a Blellow 'Follow me' button for your website but unlike (for example) Facebook and LinkedIn, this is purely an image and it's up to you to turn it into a hyperlink to your home page on the system (which will be http://blellow.com/yourusername). Presumably the equivalents of Tweetdeck and other applications (see Twitter below) will emerge if the market demands it.

Tips and tricks

- You have longer to express yourself than you would on Twitter (300 characters here), but don't waffle.

- It's a small and friendly group; depending on how quickly it grows it could be some time before you get any useful feedback for business, but it could well be a grower.

- As of mid-2009 the system is still in beta and it crashed once during the course of this book being written. These glitches should be ironed out as the network matures.

Blogger

Blogger

In 1999 a company called Pyra Labs started up doing other stuff, but it made a piece of software called Blogger. This stood for web-logger, and the idea was that people could collect links, assemble their thoughts and share them with anyone who happened along.

1999 is a lifetime ago on the Internet and Blogger, now owned by Google, has been joined by WordPress, Windows Live Spaces, TypePad and numerous other sites offering blogging and hosting combined.

What is it?

You log on, you set up an account and you blog. It really is as easy as that. You don't have to worry about setting up an RSS Feed, Blogger

does it all for you: people just click the RSS button on your blog and it starts sending your posts to their email or newsreader, whatever they want to do.

You're free to add pictures, videos, anything you wish to your blog posts as long as you think your client group will be interested. There are a number of templates available so you can make your site look businesslike, and if you buy a domain name from somewhere like easily.co.uk, then you can have it pointing straight at your blog so the customer thinks they're looking at yourblog.co.uk rather than your-blog.blogger.co.uk. Watch out, though, this can confuse search engines because you're forwarding and they might downgrade your site on their list as a result.

Who uses it?

Absolutely anyone can look at a blog hosted by the major companies outlined above. The target audience will be decided by the blogger themselves; the disadvantage of this, such as it is, is that the owner of a business-related blog might well find themselves trying to market a blog as well as their core product or service.

Don't be put off. In WordPress, for example, you're encouraged to set up links with fellow bloggers and they'll start linking to you if you're relevant. If you have something interesting to say and can start letting the social networking community know about it, people will start to pay attention. As long as your objective is branding that's great; if you're looking for increased sales then clearly the content is what's going to make the difference (do look at a few blogs, though; you'll find very few of them include overt sales messages).

What's in it for a business?

The opportunity to get your blog straight to the desktop or mobile phone of your customer and prospective customer, which is a communications tool you'll control and won't be filtered through journalists, designers or anyone else.

How to get involved

First a disclaimer: I'm focusing on Blogger here purely because it's first alphabetically. The competition logically deserves an entry in its own right, but the content of these entries would be so repetitious it wouldn't be worth the reader's while. So please take it as read that with very slight variations the following apply to WordPress and the rest of the blog-hosting sites.

Start by going to the home page at blogger.com.

You'll see they've made it really easy to register while you're in the process of starting your blog. Click 'Create Your Blog Now' and get on to the 'Create your page' section. If you have a Google account, simply use that; otherwise set up a Blogger account.

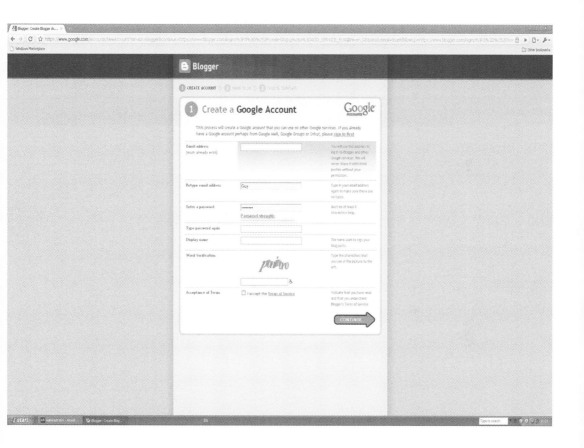

You'll be taken to a page asking you to name your blog (easy) and to give it an address on the web. This is where the headaches start, as all the best ones have gone by now. While setting up a dummy account for demonstration purposes for this book, I found that socialnetworkingblog.blogspot.com had gone, as had socialnetworking.blogspot.com; I was able to set up www. thisissocialnetworking.blogspot.com, but it's hardly catchy.

You're offered a choice of template. Click the one you want; I opted for 'Snapshot', but there's a fair selection. The blog is now created: simple as that. Press the 'Start blogging' button and you have the screen below.

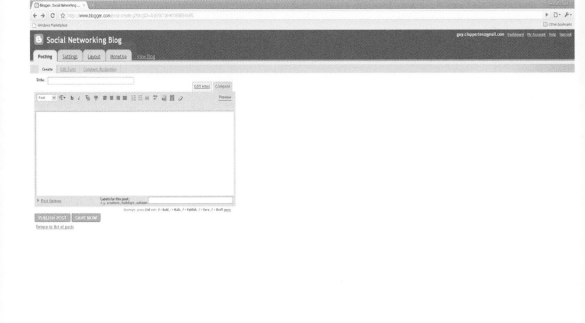

You can now just start typing if you wish; you might also want to adjust the layout. Read the 'Monetize' section for how to add Google Ads really quickly. The Layouts tab is also worth checking: look for 'Add a gadget' by which you can add pictures, adverts from Google

Search engine optimization: structuring the text and underlying code of your website so the search engines will list it prominently.

AdSense, all manner of things. You can also edit the raw HTML code of your blog, which can become very important when you're looking at factors like search engine optimization (SEO) and adding tags so that people can find you.

Play with it – there are loads of ways to make a great deal out of a blog.

Applications and add-ons

The beauty of blogging systems is that it's always possible to customize; they offer you a choice on the page. Check the 'Gadgets' box under 'Layouts' and add advertising, video, whatever you like.

Tips and tricks

- Check the section in this book on SEO and being found (Chapter 4) and make sure you're make all the right moves so that people will actually find you.

- Make sure you have something to say before you start, there's nothing worse than a dead and deserted blog.

- Think also about whether you want to be hosted or self-hosted; see the next chapter.

Delicious/Digg/ StumbleUpon

The essence of social networking is participation (that'll be the 'social' bit, he observed brilliantly) and if you want to participate then you'll need to share some stuff. This is where the sharing sites come into their own. Delicious, Digg, StumbleUpon: there are simply loads of sites that will allow you to share content with other people. Remember, though, the idea is to share content from other sites rather than your own.

This can still be useful in a business sense. You might want to bookmark something your customers will find interesting; if they get used to coming to your site for interesting bookmarks, then they're on your site regularly. What you can switch-sell them to look at after they've arrived is of course up to you.

What is it?

Naturally, all these services are different. StumbleUpon is technically a software add-on to the Firefox Internet browser, and once you've installed it and set up an account it will start sending people wherever you want them to go. You can click for other people's choices of site, too. This is more of a leisure thing than a business function; you know nothing about the other members and might not want to see their choices.

Digg focuses more on community and feedback on sites than most of the other bookmark services, and of course you don't want to spend too much professional time servicing another community. For the purposes of this chapter, then, we'll look at Delicious, simply because it's easy to set up and to add a list of useful links to your blog or website, changing them with a single click.

Who uses it?

The social sharing sites have one thing in common: their members are social types and have already bought into the idea of sharing everything useful with everyone else. This means they're ready to receive stuff from you, but they probably won't be on your Delicious account page looking for things. You need to make people aware that you've added material by shouting about it on your website; tell people you're sharing stuff, and go to http://addthis.com to get a button so that people can add your site to their own sharing network with a single click.

Stickiness is a marketing term, meaning the incentive people have to come back again and again; if the content keeps changing and you send them somewhere interesting every time they turn up, they'll keep coming back.

What's in it for a business?

Although it is primarily aimed at individuals wanting to share their interesting links, a bookmarking service can add a lot to the 'stickiness' of your website.

How to get involved

Go to http://delicious.com for a start, obviously. On the top right-hand corner, click the 'Join now' panel. You're invited to put in your first name, last name, email details and so forth, and there's a check box with text for you to identify (it cuts down on spammers).

You will then be asked to add some buttons to your web browser. This is an important step. It won't affect the smooth running of your computer and there have been no cases of anyone having their security compromised by doing this, but it's these add-ons that allow you to bookmark things and then find your bookmarks. Literally drag and drop the blue lettering up to your Internet browser's toolbar and it'll install in a split second.

You can then import any bookmarks you might already have in a file. To bookmark any website and save it to your Delicious account, simply click the 'Bookmark on Delicious' text you've just dragged to your toolbar while you have the desired page on screen. To view your bookmarks, click the 'My Delicious' text that you also dragged there.

Slightly more clever and, surprisingly, not immediately easy to find as they're buried in the 'Help' pages, are the extra little widgets you can attach to your own website to make people aware you're using the system. Log onto your Delicious account and type the address http://delicious.com/help/linkrolls and you'll find the one that I suggest is most useful. This gives you the screen below, using a dummy account I set up for the book and one bookmark (in this case the BBC News page).

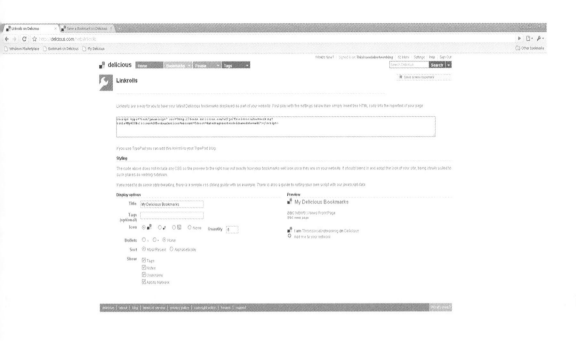

Reproduced with permission of Yahoo! Inc. ©2009 Yahoo! Inc. Delicious and the Delicious logo are registered trademarks of Yahoo! Inc.

You can see from the preview that cutting and pasting the code in the box onto my website would show a selection of my Delicious bookmarks, an exhortation to people to follow me and my Delicious user name. So people coming to my website know they'll get a look at some of the stuff I find interesting. Now, think about some of the hypothetical businesses we discussed earlier in the book, for example the ancient music specialist, who can now click a little box on her browser during her research and automatically link to material that her customers will find interesting.

Applications and add-ons

There are a number of third-party applications for Delicious and other similar sites; buttons other than the ones the companies themselves offer, aggregators that get groups of accounts displaying on the one screen. For business purposes I'd recommend keeping things simple.

Tips and tricks

- Have fun with Delicious, but remember that anything you bookmark will reflect on your business.

- Remember to keep things up to date; if it looks as though all your links are ancient your site will look dated too.

- Remember also that you don't have to share your links: you're welcome to use Delicious as a private bookmarking site and not tell anyone about it or put links on your own site. You'll be missing many of the benefits if you do this, though.

Ecademy

Ecademy has been established since 1998 and is aimed squarely at the business community. If you're selling to other businesses it could well be worth joining; if your business sells to the consumer community only I'd skip this section (and LinkedIn a little later). Ecademy's a little different from many of the other networks listed in this chapter because it doesn't perceive itself as purely dedicated to electronic networking; getting people meeting face to face and collaborating is one of its declared objectives.

What is it?

Ecademy aims to link people up and get them working together, it's as simple as that. All of its members are businesspeople and it has targeted smaller organizations in particular. A businesslike, text-based system, you need an idea of what you're doing here and why; there are fewer helpful signposts around the place than might be expected in a more consumer-friendly environment.

Who uses it?

Businesspeople only. Not that they police it particularly carefully, but anyone other than a business customer is going to lose interest in what's going on very quickly. This isn't a criticism. The design is bordering on austere, the text-only nature of the contacts is offputting for fun-seekers, the news section is targeted towards businesspeople.

Ecademy offers a network every bit as targeted as Bebo, but with a radically different target. It's also directly into competition with LinkedIn, as we'll see a little later. The drawback with Ecademy is that you're asked to pay for a number of services that other networks offer free of charge.

What's in it for a business?

There's a rigidly defined set of fellow networkers and little waffle on the site. The come-ons for money are atypical of social networking but may be a sign of what's coming; there's a debate about just how long this stuff can stay free for.

How to get involved

The opening screen couldn't be clearer. There is no messing about on details of how wonderful the website is, you just join up on the home page.

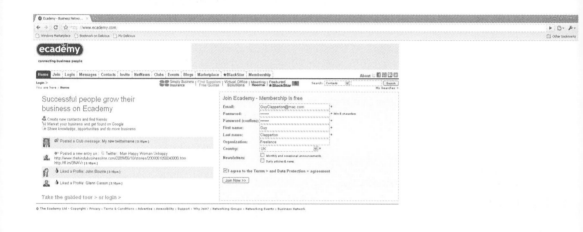

You'll then receive a code that you can cut and paste into the next screen, and alternately a link to click on: either of those things will confirm your membership of the network.

The first thing you're invited to do is to ask other people to join; this, as in the other examples that ask you for the same thing, is an attempt to grow the business. Don't think for a minute that you're obliged to nominate colleagues unless you think they'd be pleased.

On the left-hand side of the page just after you've logged in you'll find a number of options. The first thing to do is to click on your profile. The site doesn't let you at it immediately but offers you a range of paid services, including having your profile searchable on Google and the right to start a blog (for PowerNetworkers, £11.95 a month as this book went to print).

You may have noticed that Google submission and the right to start as many blogs as you want are free on such blogging systems as WordPress and Windows Live.

What's in a name?

OK, so why should you want to pay for an Ecademy blog when you can get them free from elsewhere? There may actually be some good reasons. If you're a professional company selling goods or services to blue-chip clients, the idea of having an obvious off-the-shelf blog address might not appeal to you. You may wish to make the statement implicit in paying for a blog that you care a little more about your image. I think you're crazy, but it matters to some.

Further charges apply to people wanting extra analytics and the ability to drum up more business in a targeted way. We'll assume that you want the free version for the moment. Click the 'No thanks, I'll take free membership' button and it takes you to another screen where you can complete your profile (which actually we asked to do two screens ago, but never mind).

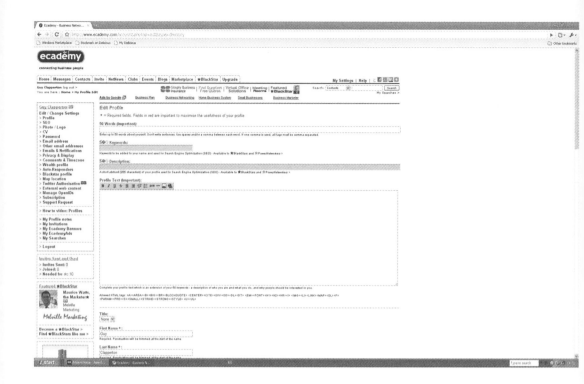

The screen helps you through the process by highlighting the bits that are really going to matter in red. Type in your profile, then save it. There is also a link on the left of the page to help you manage keywords and SEO, and also to links and banners for your website (note: some of these have more to do with Ecademy advertising than anything else).

There is then the option to look at your messages, but above all to join 'clubs' and start interacting with other members with the same interests. This is where the interaction really starts.

Applications and add-ons

Ecademy is pretty much a self-contained site, and other than banners for your own site there isn't a lot that's going to add any significant value to your experience of it.

Tips and tricks

- Lurk for a while and get the hang of what the other members are likely to expect before launching in with a service or sales pitch.

- Join a few clubs and interest groups; you might well make some interesting contacts.

- Don't be too critical because the company feels it has to charge for its services. As recently as June 2009 there was speculation that all of these companies would eventually have to charge, or else why run a social network? If Ecademy has simply pulled ahead of the pack and submitted to the inevitable, fair enough. You charge for what you do, after all. LinkedIn also has a paid-for premium version and at the time of writing there were rumours that Twitter would be launching one as well.

Facebook

Facebook was arguably the site that got social networking moving in the first place. In spite of what I said in the introduction, during which we discussed how Cix, Compuserve and others had started way before it was called social networking, it was only once a large number of people had broadband Internet connections that the idea became widely accepted. Facebook's rise more or less coincided with the social media revolution.

In spite of what you've heard about Twitter in the press, Facebook remains the largest social network to date in terms of sheer numbers.

There is a greater opportunity to talk to more people here than anywhere else, if you know what you're doing.

What is it?

Facebook began as an academic idea, as indeed did the Internet itself. Facebook was intended to keep alumni of a college in touch with each other when they didn't have the time to stay in touch properly. It soon spread beyond academia and supplanted a number of paid-for means of keeping in touch with old colleagues, however. Following this it moved outside colleges all together and is now used by huge numbers of people trying to keep in touch.

The updates you're likely to put up are normally text only. There will be room for people to comment on these updates once they've adopted you as a 'friend'. You'll have the opportunity to put video and photo content on the site as well, and the chance to exchange private as well as public messages.

Essentially Facebook is one of the more complex social networking environments, but potentially very rewarding once you really have its strengths and weaknesses straight in your mind.

Who uses it?

As with a lot of social networking sites, the surprise for people with preconceptions about who's using this stuff is that the fastest-growing group on Facebook as at 2009 was the middle aged and indeed the elderly. The number of 35–44 year olds grew 276.4 percent in the six months to April 2009, while the 55+ market grew 194.3 percent over the same period; 55 per cent of users are female. The source of this information was www.istrategylabs.com, which revisits the research every six months, so if you want a really up-to-date picture, check it online.

There are a couple of things of which you can be reasonably certain on Facebook. First, it has a lot more bells and whistles – or complications, as some people might call them – than Twitter. This means that a real computer novice is likely to be slightly put off. Second, though, the vast number of people who do get there are going to be more inclined to spend some time on the site, whether looking at some of the messages, updating their status or playing one of the many games available. There are clear opportunities for a business wanting to promote itself through, say, a branded game, or taking out an advertisement on the site. More people, more eye time, more branding. Simple.

What's in it for a business?

Facebook is the largest social network and the one of which your customers are most likely to be members already. If you decide social networking is for you, then it won't be a matter of 'Have you got a Facebook Group' but 'Why aren't you on Facebook?'

How to get involved

Like a lot of the networks under discussion, getting onto Facebook is simple. Go to www.facebook.com and enter your name, address and email details where prompted. You'll get a confirmation email to say you've joined. Click the link on the email and you're in.

You can now log on using your name and password. The next thing to do is to set up your profile so that people can get the hang of who you are. This might not be as straightforward as it sounds, as there is a lot of information to choose from.

The first section, basic information, is as it says on the tin, basic, but watch it. Declare your sex, OK, people will see that from your picture, but remember to hide your date of birth (you can do that from a drop-down box) – identity thieves are watching and the more information you've made public the easier it is for them. Home town and home neighbourhood, again, I'd avoid unless you're talking about business premises. Political views, marital status, religious views and whether you're interested in men, women or dating are likewise going to be irrelevant; leave the free text bits blank and click 'Networking' only.

The next stage is 'Personal information'; hobbies, interests, favourite films, that sort of thing. If you want friends to get in touch with you that's fine; if you want to keep your profile businesslike then your collection of Osmonds records is your business and no one else's. Contact information, the next tab, is also worth watching for privacy breaches, although if you haven't gone ex-directory it would be absurd to withhold your phone number from Facebook; your education experience is likewise nobody's business but your own unless you choose to share it. I really don't want to sound alarmist, but public information on Facebook really can be a goldmine for identity thieves.

At this stage the temptation is to start playing around with all the 'harmless' little bits of code and games you're offered, but my advice is don't. I did: let me make that mistake for you. A load of fellow journalists said they'd started playing a game called 'Zombies', which consists largely of sending messages to people saying you've been chomped by a zombie. Worse, it appears on your home page: 'Guy Clapperton has been chomped by a zombie', it says. Worse is the 'Compare people' application, a game that lets your friends rate your best qualities. I'm pleased to say I came out as a good listener, reliable...and I get a monthly email saying that none of my female friends wants to date me. Oh, and apparently I'm more like Patrick Troughton, the second Doctor Who, than any of the others, and there's a list of books I've read and intend to read.

For a freelance it's not so bad to be thought of as a little frivolous from time to time. For other businesses – say you were an undertaker – it could be very bad indeed. My suggestion would be to do a search for people you know or for your customers and add them to your list – they'll have to approve this – then watch their updates. If they're serious users then you can start a Facebook group: upload your logo, hit 'Start a group' and the site opens a closed area for you. You can then invite people to join the group, and they can share ideas and thoughts.

Be careful. The thoughts about your business they want to share may be negative. Or no one may want to join, and nothing looks worse for you than a Facebook group without any participants. The other thing Facebook will do is suggest people for you to add to your friends list and it has some strange ideas as to why you'd be interested. It's offered me several people as 'friends' I probably know because, well, they live in London too.

Applications and add-ons

There are a number of technical additions that can make Facebook a little simpler for the user. If you want to keep up with your friends' (or customers', or competitors') updates but don't want to be on Facebook the whole time, have a look at Seesmic (www.seesmic.com) and download it. It reads the messages and presents them to you in a small box. Tweetdeck (www.tweetdeck.com) will do the same with both Facebook and the people you're following on

Twitter. You can use this to synchronize your tweets and updates as well.

There are a huge number of games and applications that Facebook itself makes available to you. The vast majority are aimed at the leisure user rather than the business user so watch out; they can take up a lot of your time.

Tips and tricks

- Facebook was invented as a social application; don't be surprised when it turns out not to be designed for business use.

- As this book went to press, Facebook bought FriendFeed (see the next entry). It also launched a sort of 'Facebook Lite', which looked a lot like a Twitter competitor.

- If you're setting up a Facebook group, don't underestimate the time and effort it's going to take to supervise it and pull together some sort of online community. These things don't just happen, much though we might all wish they did!

Friendfeed

Friendfeed, recently bought by Facebook, has taken some of the more popular features of other social networking sites and come out with something slightly different. Aimed at the consumer or small business, it can be a flexible way of working on a document within your organization as well as getting new customers or communicating with existing ones.

What is it?

Friendfeed is one of those networks that's really got the hang of internetworking with other log-ins. Far from competing with Twitter and Facebook, it allows you to use your Twitter, Facebook or Google log-in to join the service. I used Twitter; it asked for my Twitter log-on, then checked again that it was OK to use it, then started reading my Twitter feed for me. It also checked my Facebook contacts when I asked it to and I have no doubt it would do the same with my Googlemail contacts as well.

Who uses it?

According to data from Quantcast, Friendfeed appeals to a predominantly young audience that's slightly male dominated, 45–55 percent compared to 10 percent female. The audience also likes gaming websites.

Aggregation: bringing feeds from a number of social networks and displaying them on one screen.

What's in it for a business?

It's a convenient way of aggregating and sorting out a selection of different news and information feeds.

How to get involved

If you're a member of Googlemail, Twitter or Facebook already, then by far the easiest way of joining is to use one of these log-ons. Friendfeed will import and aggregate as many of your contacts as you want, in a constantly updated stream that looks a lot like a Twitter feed.

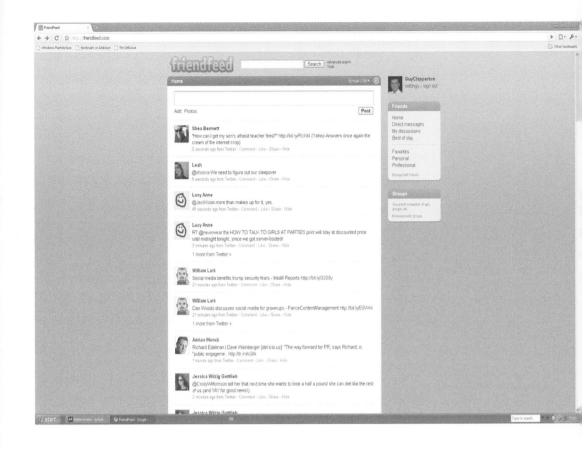

The extra value it offers lies both in bringing the feeds together (hence the name, I guess!) and in the ability to start and join groups. The 'Groups' link on the right of the page allows you to join interest groups, comment on what they're looking at and doing and – as long as you do it subtly and add some sort of value – mention that you're an expert in a given field, or that you sell something in which the people in the group might be interested.

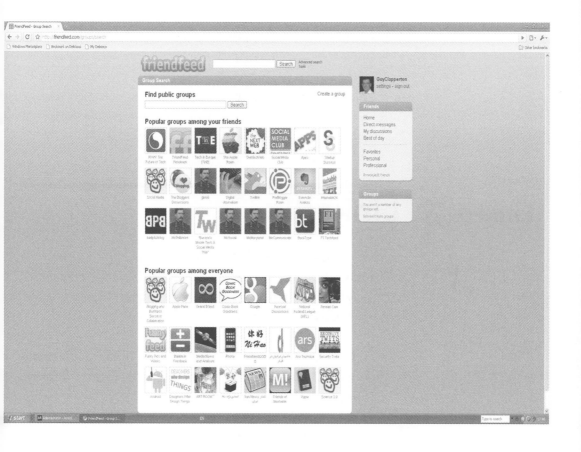

You can also create a group. This can be closed, so your staff can join and use it as a closed intranet within your organization.

Applications and add-ons

None: Friendfeed itself is like an add-on to a number of other networks.

Tips and tricks

- The groups have a handy guide to how many posts they receive on average, so if you join one with about six posts a day you can be certain there won't be any major overhead in keeping up with it.

- As this book went to press, Facebook bought Friendfeed. Neither company had announced how this would affect the service but you can be sure it'll be folded into Facebook somehow.

Linked in.   # LinkedIn

LinkedIn predates both Twitter and Facebook and if you're in the business-to-business sector then it's a must. If you sell primarily to consumers, then they're less likely to be interested in joining a purpose-built business network.

One of the prime features of LinkedIn is that it involves a bit more work in terms of searching people out and making contact with them. It is down to you to make contact with people and to make it work. That said, the people who are involved are much more likely to be in listening mode for business proposals. They'll have had you recommended to them by one of their colleagues (you can't just look them up and send a proposal, you need to be endorsed by one of your contacts who's also on LinkedIn).

What is it?

Anyone who has heard the old adage about everyone being connected to actor Kevin Bacon by six degrees of separation will understand the principle that sparked LinkedIn off. It wasn't a group thing like Facebook and the others, it was a matter of joining and inviting contacts to join, who'd then do the same and see who they knew. Eventually the scheme grew so that if you were interested in talking to someone interesting – say me – you could see whether I was on LinkedIn, then see whether a colleague of a colleague of a colleague knew me. You then put in a request for an introduction.

It has evolved since then: you can update your status just as you can with Twitter and Facebook, and you can start discussion groups.

Who uses it?

LinkedIn is a business-only site. This has several advantages, not least of which is that people getting a contact through it are expecting to be tapped for favours or to receive a sales pitch. According to recent figures from Techcrunch, the demographic is about 64 percent male and the average age is 41; you can imagine the sex balance evening out and the age lowering gradually as a generation accustomed to living and breathing social networking gets older.

What's in it for a business?

LinkedIn is a ready-made business network including high-value individuals, with no waffle and no charges.

How do I get involved?

By now you'll know the basic routine: sign up, set up an account and fill in your profile, remembering that you're in a professional rather than a personal environment.

Of all of the social networks, LinkedIn probably takes up the most work because you have to actively look for people who're going to interest you, and make requests to contact them through intermediaries. Once you've taken the trouble, the personal response you're likely to get more than makes up for this.

The process is pretty simple: you search for the name of a person you want to contact and if they're on LinkedIn, the system tells you how many degrees of separation there are between you and that person. So you send a contact message – the content is up to you – and this goes to the person you know, asking them to forward it, then they forward it to the person they know, and so on until it gets to the person you want to contact.

That's the service with which it launched, but the site has grown. You can now start a LinkedIn group, either for your company or for a professional interest group. The following is a sample LinkedIn prepared earlier by way of illustration, concerning its own business.

Linked in ® People ▾ | Jobs ▾ | Answers ▾ | Companies ▾   Account & Settings | Help | Sign Out   Language ▾

Explore People Search: Director at Apple - Internet (Silicon Valley) - VP Operations   **Search Companies** ▾ [   ] **Search**

Companies `BETA`   Companies Home | Add Company | FAQ

LinkedIn

Last edited by
Associate Marketing Manager
Edit profile

LinkedIn takes your professional network online,
giving you access to people, jobs and opportunities   **Linked in** ®
like never before. Built upon trusted connections and relationships,
LinkedIn has established the world's largest and most powerful
professional network. Currently, more than 40 million professionals are on
LinkedIn, including executives from all five hundred of the Fortune
500... see more

Specialties
Online Professional Network, Jobs, Events, Research, People Search,
Professional Identity

Current Employees (479 total, 479 in your network)
- Patti Mae Bey, Ad Operations Specialist
- Steve Pecko, Creative & Campaign Manager, Enterprise Marketing
- Jeff Weiner, President
- Amber Mercado, Client Services Representative
- Alvin Adlawan, Network Support Specialist

See more »

Former Employees
- **Shannon Edwards**, Director, ShopStyle Europe at Sugar
  Interim Director, PR & Marketing, Europe (to May 2008)
- **Kirtley Wienbroer**, Founder at Integrated Sprockets
  Architect, Corporate IT (to September 2008)
- **Jia Jiang**, MBA Candidate at Duke University - Fuqua School of
  Business
  MBA Intern - International Marketing Manager (to August 2008)
- **Holly Jin**, Chief Scientist at Cardinal Optimization Inc
  Analytics Researcher (to July 2008)
- **Al Rey**, Experienced Social Media Professional
  Account Executive, Corporate Solutions (to May 2009)

New Hires
- **Matt Warburton**, Interim Director of Enterprise Community Marketing
  was Director of Community Management at Yahoo! - 2 months ago
- **Kim Kochaver**, Director, Advertising Trade Marketing
  was Marketing Director at Federated Media - 2 months ago
- **Francois Dufour**, Sr. Director, Enterprise Marketing
  was Director, Product Marketing at Yahoo! - 4 months ago

Related Companies

Career path for LinkedIn employees
before: after:
- Yahoo!   - Google
- PayPal   - Facebook

LinkedIn employees are most connected to:
- 23andMe
- PayPal
- GiftCertificates.com
- IrisLogic

See more »

Key Statistics

Top Locations
- San Francisco Bay Area (269)
- Greater Omaha Area (48)
- London, United Kingdom (15)
- Greater New York City Area (13)

▸ Headquarters Address

Headquarters	San Francisco Bay Area
Industry	Internet
Type	Privately Held
Status	Operating
Company Size	350 employees
Website	http://www.linkedin.com

Common Job Titles	Senior Software Engineer	10%
	Software Engineer	8%
	Account Executive	3%
	Account Manager	3%
	Web Developer	3%
Top Schools	Stanford Univ.	6%
	San Jose St. Univ.	5%
	Univ. of Nebraska at Omaha	4%
Median Age	33 years	

Left sidebar

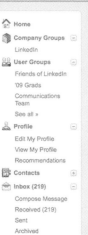

🏠 **Home**
📋 **Company Groups** ⊟
   LinkedIn
👥 **User Groups** ⊟
   Friends of LinkedIn
   '09 Grads
   Communications Team
   See all »
👤 **Profile** ⊟
   Edit My Profile
   View My Profile
   Recommendations
📇 **Contacts** ⊟
📧 **Inbox (219)** ⊟
   Compose Message
   Received (219)
   Sent
   Archived
📱 **Applications** ⊟
   Reading List by Amazon
   Events
   My Travel
   Company Buzz
   Blog Link
   Huddle Workspaces
   Box.net Files

Add Connections

Krista Canfield

Career Expert and
Spokesperson for LinkedIn

Krista is always looking for
stellar new co-workers. Let
me know if you know some
great candidates!
http://ping.fm/ZCIY0
4 hours ago [Edit]

It's also worth mentioning that LinkedIn not only allows you to build up a profile, as you can see from the column on the left, but you can leave a recommendation for someone with whom you've worked and they can leave recommendations for you.

Applications and add-ons

It's possible to link updates from LinkedIn with those from other networks, but I really wouldn't. Mixing updates is now handled very easily by the Yoono add-on (I promise I am not making these names up) to the Firefox web browser, but the cultures are very different: LinkedIn users won't expect the personal stuff you're likely to add to Facebook, and Facebook members in turn don't appreciate the sheer number of updates that come their way if you've linked your Twitter account and want to keep the two in sync.

Like many of the sites and networks discussed in this chapter, LinkedIn allows you to link to your profile from your own website. So it's possible to get a sort of extended CV online with recommendations and references already built in from people with whom you've worked, which people can find with a single click from your usual site. For professionals this is likely to be much more useful than, for example, a Facebook page.

Tips and tricks

● Remember that LinkedIn's a business network and be flexible about moving business matters onto it. A colleague of mine started a group for technology PR people and journalists on Facebook and found hardly anyone turned up; she moved it to LinkedIn and within days it was a lively forum because that's where people expected to go for work-related items.

- By the same token, don't choke up your LinkedIn profile with irrelevant updates. It's a work thing and nobody on this network wants to know what you had for breakfast.

- Take the time to seek people out through mutual connections. LinkedIn can provide a quasi-vetting process, by which the people between you and your contact will filter out time wasters so they'll probably take you seriously when your contact message arrives.

MySpace

MySpace is often dismissed in the media as the one that came before Facebook and Twitter, but don't write it off; in America alone it had more than 60 million regular members as this book went to print. Granted, a few months earlier it was closer to 70 million, but if your services or goods are aimed at young people who upload music and video and want a forum on which to discuss it, that's a hell of a sizeable lump of people to risk ignoring.

What is it?

MySpace shares much in common with YouTube on the surface, in that you can share a great deal of content such as music and videos. There are offers of tickets to gigs, ads for the latest movies (often with loud sounds; don't go to MySpace in a busy office without headphones unless you can justify it, as your writer found out when a voice explaining there was a new Terminator film issued forth on his first log-in).

The network's own blurb maintains there is space for business networking on MySpace; technically there is no reason why not, but the garish colours and layouts militate against this more than slightly.

A major difference between MySpace and YouTube, however, is the scope for building and moderating discussion groups. If you doubt whether this is particularly important, bear in mind the success of the Arctic Monkeys, a rock group that shot to public fame through MySpace before they became major recording artists. It remains a powerful network and if your business promotes entertainment to young people, you should consider trying to harness it.

Who uses it?

The demographics in independent studies suggest that the membership of MySpace is getting older and that the environment is therefore likely to start looking more mature as a result. It's difficult to see much evidence of this from the site itself, which still has exhortations to see the latest videos, listen to the latest music and chat about it all in the newest forums, splashed across its front pages.

This might sound like a criticism, which isn't my intention – in a business book this is going to make it less appropriate for many readers. Had I been writing a different sort of book this would be evidence of how MySpace is getting things spectacularly right.

What's in it for a business?

There's a ready audience of young people who are ready and receptive for the 'next big thing'. Beware, though: clearly, for every Arctic Monkeys there's another 50 groups who've done less well.

How do I get involved?

The sign-up process is similar to most of the social networks except that MySpace offers special sign-ups for comedians and musicians, once again emphasizing the entertainment orientation of this network. Once you have signed up, the structure of the opening page tells you a lot about what to expect from MySpace.

As well as the standard 'here are your new friends' message, including the CEO of MySpace (he is a compulsory friend for new members of MySpace), there is a selection of videos and a highlighted personality before anyone has even filled in a profile.

Instant messaging:
E-mail-like system that allows you to send a message to anyone using the same messaging service, for example Windows Live! Instant Messenger.

There is also a clear encouragement to upload music and videos and an automatic start-up of an instant messaging client, as well the opportunity to start a blog.

For the diehard business user this is likely to be too much at once; for the target customer this everything-in-one-place might be perfect, although they're just as likely to want to upload a video to YouTube, put a blog on Blogger or WordPress and mix and match: they are becoming more sophisticated.

There is also a lively forum section. This offers businesses the chance to offer value to the audience; if an organization isn't certain it will attract enough people to its own Facebook page, a selection of forums like this one might make a viable alternative to join in order to establish some sort of thought leadership in a given area.

Applications and add-ons

There are very few add-ons, although a mobile version of MySpace is available for download. The idea of MySpace is to get people online and using it as their home; the advertising that is sold on the strength of the time people spend online is how the site makes its money.

Tips and tricks

- You need to be in tune with the MySpace culture to make your time worthwhile on this one; it's not going to change and it's not going to react well to a 'stuffed shirt'.

- If your target customer isn't exactly right for the MySpace environment, don't try to send them there; they won't go.

- Social networks are subject to fashion fluctuations; although MySpace still has millions of members, it doesn't have as many millions as it did a few years ago. It's certainly not on the critical list, but it could be worth Googling 'MySpace demographic' before committing to a marketing campaign on it in the future. For all anyone knows it could be the next in-thing again within months!

Picasa

Picasa should by rights be a subsection within Blogger, because it's an application that sits on your computer – it's a free download – but you then get to upload your pictures to http://picasaweb.google.com. You can organize them, set security levels, put them into different albums and make them available or not to whomever you want. As you'll gather from the address, it's owned by Google and its appeal is as widespread.

An application is a piece of software that does something, so Microsoft Word is an application, while Microsoft Windows is an operating system because it's an environment on which you put applications.

What is it?

Quite simply, Picasa is a piece of software linked to a secure website that allows you to manage your photos online, either for your personal and business use or to share in public. As a Google product you can imagine it's fairly well linked to Blogger.

Who uses it?

An even spread of men and women, predominantly over 50, but you don't need to know this: unusually in this section you're not being invited to join a community, just organize your own stuff and conceivably browse other people's pictures.

What's in it for a business?

Any business that needs photography can benefit from Picasa and other services like Flickr (see the tips and tricks section). An estate agent can have photographs available when out of the office, using a mobile device; in fact, anyone using photography in their business would do well to have a look at this software.

How do I get involved?

At the risk of cutting a section short, sign in using a Google ID and start uploading by hitting the 'Upload photographs now' button. It's genuinely as easy as that.

Applications and add-ons

Picasa is itself an add-on, so none.

Tips and tricks

- If you'd rather use a website than an application for the same kind of function, have a look at www.flickr.com, which allows for the upload, online management and sharing of pictures.

- Need a picture for a brochure or website? My journalist glands are saying 'stop putting photographers out of work, commission something!' but you might not have the budget. Check http://picasaweb.google.com/lh/explore# and don't forget to look at the copyright disclaimers. Look also at Flickr.com; there might well be a photo someone has put up there specifically for people to share. Even if there's no copyright attached, please, please credit the photographer.

ⓟ plaxo Plaxo

Plaxo was one of the earliest social networks, starting in the 1990s as an online contact directory so you'd never need to type them all into an address book again. The initial reaction was hostile; people didn't understand that someone would offer a service like this without harvesting the addresses and selling them on. True to its word, Plaxo did no such thing and has grown to expand its offering with the Plaxo Pulse, an update system that is close to (but not exactly the same as) a LinkedIn, Facebook or Twitter update.

What is it?

At base, Plaxo remains a neat way of keeping all of your contacts up to date; you enter their details or upload them from your Outlook file, and it mails the people periodically to ask if the information is still up to date.

It's also an update/message system that allows you to post brief messages about what you're doing at any given time. In addition to this, Plaxo has dabbled in 'fan pages' and groups, like a lot of the social networking providers, but the fan groups appear to be small (for example, the *Star Trek* fan page – Trekkies being very active in forums throughout the Internet – had 64 'shares' one month after the 2009 movie came out).

One of its main points of value, and Wikipedia backs this view up, is as an aggregator of content from other networks. The fan pages are powered by Fancast and many people with Plaxo accounts share their updates from Twitter, Facebook, LinkedIn or wherever else they happen to be on the web.

Who uses it?

Ignite Social Media reports that Plaxo has an even spread of male and female users, and more of them have a bachelor's degree than not. They are almost all over 35.

What's in it for a business?

In spite of Plaxo's determination to market itself as a bona fide social network, the updating/sharing idea is so widely available on bigger networks it's almost not worth mentioning. Where Plaxo is brilliant is in its directory service: download whichever of the add-ons will work with your address book (there's one on the downloads tab for Outlook, one for Apple's address book and so on) and it keeps your address book up to date, periodically asking the people in it to update their own entries. In this it's unique, if they bother updating!

How do I get involved?

A very straightforward sign-up process is followed (ideally) by downloading the address book application. This uploads your contacts and asks those people whether they're still where you think they are, they amend accordingly and your address book is up to date.

By all means look at joining groups on Plaxo; this is an area that may grow, but the signs at the moment are that there is a limited audience using these. People wanting discussions are gravitating towards blogs, Facebook and other higher-profile networks.

Applications and add-ons

The main value of the Plaxo network is in the applications available on the downloads page. There are also third-party applications that will link all of your updates – Plaxo Pulse, Twitter, Facebook – but beware of doing this too freely. As I've mentioned elsewhere, people have different expectations on different networks, and you might alienate your Facebook 'friends' by sending them all of your tweets and dominating their home page.

Tips and tricks

- A number of colleagues might still find the idea of Plaxo having all of their details undesirable. The brand has proven to be trustworthy and protective of private data over time, but if someone wants you to take their details down, they're within their rights.

- A related matter is that as a business, you may need to take advice on data protection legislation before sharing people's data with Plaxo or any other online database.

Twitter

As I write, Twitter is the bees' knees, the head honcho, the granddaddy of them all (except it's one of the newest). Well, it is if you could column inches and percentage growth; in fact Facebook has a larger number of users and far richer content.

None of that matters to you; the situation can all change overnight. What you need to know is whether Twitter's going to be any use to you. The way you find this out is to do a quick audit of your customers and prospects before you even think about using it. Are they already on Twitter? Are they thinking of joining it? OK, then have a look at joining yourself.

What is it?

Twitter at its most basic is a series of 140-character announcements to anyone who happens to be reading. These announcements are called 'tweets'. It's really as simple as that, and the simplicity is what makes it work.

Twitter didn't catch on immediately. Its founders put the service on a web page and let people make their announcements. From these I could gather that a lot of people had breakfast in the morning, and by lunchtime they were ready for lunch. In the evenings they would on average have whatever they called the evening meal, then later on they'd go to bed. This wasn't entirely thrilling.

Eventually, though, people started to put more interesting stuff up and the founders allowed a little more interaction. Crucially, they allowed people to reply to a tweet. This suddenly became a lot more involving. Consider the technology support person who puts up a tweet saying:

> *Just finished sorting out someone's Mac problem, saved them buying a new computer.*

Someone else sees this and knows they have a problem with their own Apple computer. Mac support being scarcer than PC support, they reply:

> @ITsupportperson
> Do you support Macs?
> Whereabouts are you based?

With a bit of luck the two will take this to private messages immediately so as not to bother everyone else with it. If they think their chat is going to be interesting, they'll leave it public.

The service itself is text only and free of charge. If you link to a video or audio, then some web browsers with add-ons will make your tweet look like it has the media embedded in it.

Who uses it?

The audience for Twitter is growing and evolving all the time. A few celebrities famously hang out there and share their thoughts with the world. Some are extremely skilled at this: Philip Schofield looks like a nice guy sharing words and pictures with people, but he's also incredibly clever at extending his reach to his audience and building their loyalty to his programmes. This has no impact on his being a nice guy, I should add! Some are less so; one or two comedians putting up highly unfunny comments could do worse than to give it up.

The point is that these people attract a lot of ordinary onlookers whom it's difficult to categorise. Statistics show that there are a lot more of the 35–45 age group than many people would guess; data from Hitwise in March 2009 suggested that middle-aged men were the largest constituency, whereas data from marketing research company Compete the following month said that 18–24 year olds were still the biggest users. Anecdotally, it appears there are a lot of small business owner/managers and many public relations executives and journalists on Twitter, although this perception could be skewed by the number of PR people electing to 'follow' me as a journalist.

What's in it for a business?

Twitter offers an unparalleled opportunity to react to customers sounding off in public; any announcements you might want to make have immediacy, and could well go straight to your customer's mobile phone no matter where they are; it is really simple to use.

How to get involved

Signing up to Twitter is really simple. Follow these steps:

- Go to http://twitter.com.

- Click the 'Sign up' tab.

- Enter some details.

- Start tweeting.

This gets you onto the very basic web view of Twitter, with which you're likely to become frustrated quite quickly; more on that in a moment. The next stage is to find some people to follow. Following is when you find people in whom you're interested, click on their profile and follow them. Their updates will start to appear on your Twitter web page (http://twitter.com/yourtwitternamegoeshere).

The next question is, of course, how to find relevant people, and this is a tricky one. It tends to grow organically: someone makes a comment after one of your tweets (your home page will have all of the @yourname comments as well as your own and those of the people you follow) and you find it interesting; you start following them. You hear from a friend that there's someone interesting you should follow, so you do so. There's a tradition called Followfriday in which people recommend other Twitter members to their followers because they like sharing fun or informative contacts. You feel obliged to follow Stephen Fry because it's like national service, you just think you ought to do it.

Your list of followers will soon start to grow, and they'll start recommending you to other people. There are third-party applications that will make your followers grow artificially, too, by locating people in your field and auto-adding them. We'll come on to them in a second.

Applications and add-ons

What really makes Twitter fly is the stuff that you can add to it. At base, Twitter is a web-based series of announcements. This is only so much use to business customers, who'll want their tweets categorized and prioritized.

One way of doing this is a program called Tweetdeck, which you can use on a Mac or a PC. You can find it at www.tweetdeck.com and it's fast to download. It gives you a view of your standard inbox, but also a separate column for your direct messages and another for replies and mentions. A fourth column you can configure yourself, for searches, for groups, for hashtag subjects, for anything. It's a great way to organize all of your tweets coming in, which otherwise gets a bit like juggling flour.

There are a number of other Twitter applications that will do some of the same things. Twihrl (www.twihrl.com) is one; Twitterific is somewhat simpler and works just like an offline reader for your tweets (in other words, it presents them to you in a little on-screen box rather than insisting you go through the web).

There's other stuff you can do as well. Twitpic.com is a site that lets you enter your Twitter username and password, then upload pics and automatically tweet a link to them. If you're an estate agent and you're not salivating at the thought of alerting all of your clients to a new des res and having them click through to a photo of it really, really easily, then you're not thinking. Powertwitter is an add-on for your web browser that adds a powerful search facility to your Twitter homepage, translates all the links on people's Tweets into previews and other functions.

There are yet others, and by the time you've held this book in your hand for five minutes someone will have invented even more. Twittergrader will tell you, if you enter your Twitter name, how important it thinks you are (I'm two thousandth out of 2 million, it says here, and my Twitter grading is 99.8 percent. You will have noticed this is completely meaningless ego-driven guff, I trust). Twilerts (www.twilert.com) allow you to enter a search, save it and have the updated results delivered to you periodically; so if you want to keep an eye on what people are saying about your company every week, set up a weekly twilert for yourcompanyname and you'll get a note telling you about it. The latest version of Tweetdeck will also save searches for you.

There will be more on applications with which you can use Twitter later in the book under mobile social networking. Meanwhile, we're going to have to move on or we'll be here all day.

Tips and tricks

- Remember, this is social media, so try to engage a little rather than simply putting ads up for your company; people will soon unfollow you if they think that's all they're going to get.

- If you're getting into an exchange of views with someone, consider taking it to private messages so it doesn't clutter up everybody else's in-box.

- Don't get all insecure about how many followers you have or constantly tweet about it: you'll look like a 12 year old. Or Ashton Kutcher.

- Do link to your blog from time to time, but only if it's relevant, and don't *just* post links.

- Do share stuff you find interesting.

- Don't link every tweet to an identical entry on Facebook; that's so last year.

- Try to be even shorter than 140 characters in every tweet. If I write something and someone wants to retweet it, they have to do so, with 'rt @guyclapperton' in front; that's 16 characters gone, 17 with a space afterwards. So if I'm hoping to be retweeted I try to limit my tweet to 123 characters.

- Expect to miss tweets and don't worry about it. It's going to happen. People will miss your tweets as well. It's that sort of medium.

Wikipedia

OK, this one's cheating a bit; Wikipedia isn't a social network as such, but it certainly uses social networking techniques to keep itself up to date.

Wikipedia is an online encyclopedia. What is unique about it is that it is managed by its community: you can amend entries yourself by becoming a registered user. This can be useful when you have specialist knowledge the established writers lack: for example, a colleague of mine who was a science fiction writer died a couple of years ago and I was able to amend his Wikipedia entry to reflect that he was also a popular and respected technology journalist. The facility to change entries can also be abused and it can take time for the volunteer editors to amend inaccuracies. This is why, briefly, while he was Prime Minister, Tony Blair's middle name was listed in Wikipedia as Whoop-de-do. No, it wasn't me. But if I'd thought of it first...

There's no obvious business application for Wikipedia itself, but it's possible to use the same model to build up your company's internal knowledge base, putting some sort of social networking capability into your own business. For example some engineering firms have an internal Wiki to which their employees add information based on experience as they acquire it.

YouTube

Google-owned YouTube is an interesting example of a medium that has transformed during the writing of this book. The principle is really easy: you upload videos to share with other people and that's about it.

It used to be seen primarily as a young person's medium. Then in December 2008 the Queen put her Christmas message on YouTube. In early 2009 Prime Minister Gordon Brown made an announcement about MPs' pay on YouTube; you might remember the pictures of that interesting smile, if I can put it like that. A lot of people were using the site to listen to music and watch videos, but in late 2008 a falling-out between YouTube owner Google and the rights holders meant these were all taken off, at least temporarily. These videos were reinstated as this book went to press.

Where does YouTube go next? I don't know.

What is it?

YouTube started life as, and remains, a video service. To use the site you'll need to have your video ready, preferably in MP4 format (most hard disk-based video cameras will record in this format by default). Uploading high-definition videos is fine.

URL: Universal Resource Locator, more often called a web address these days.

Your use can be a little more flexible than simply putting a video up and asking everyone to go to YouTube to look at it, though. You can upload a video and then, while you're playing it back online to check it looks OK, look to the right of the picture and you'll see a box with two pieces of code. One of these is the URL. You can put this as a link on your website and send people to the video using it.

Better still, there's an 'embed' code. Cut and paste this onto your website, making absolutely sure you paste it as plain text, and – wait for it – the video appears on your own website or blog as if you'd put it there yourself *and you don't have to pay for storing the video.* Doing so is free, and a video on your site will look very professional (temporarily, once everybody realizes how easy it is they'll all be doing it).

How to get involved

Once you've made a video – maybe a training video, maybe a piece of viral marketing, maybe a corporate presentation – set up a YouTube channel. These are free. Simply go to YouTube.com, press the 'Sign up' button, follow the instructions and enter your details. Then select a video from those on your computer to upload and start either embedding or directing people to individual videos or your YouTube channel.

Viral marketing: a piece of marketing collateral, often a video, that spreads by personal recommendation.

Inevitably, the part that will need the most work and thought is going to be making the video in the first place. Modern versions of Windows and Apple computers have excellent, easy video-editing tools on them and some copyright-free background music. Try to remember that looking flash isn't necessarily a good thing; if you use a different transition between every scene your video's going to look tacky, and if you're of the persuasion that you should use as many fonts and colours as your computer will allow then it's time you got over it.

Applications and add-ons

None – the trick with YouTube is that you can add videos from it to your own website. On the right of the screen when you're watching a video you may notice there is an area with some code – one of these codes allows you to link to the video, the other allows you to 'embed'.

Put this code into your web page as plain text and the video will appear on it as if it were on your actual site.

Tips and tricks

- Simple is good – people might be watching on their mobile devices so no matter how good your movie is they won't see fine detail

- Short is good – people don't expect to watch a video at their desk for as long as they would on a TV screen

- Passworded is easy, so if you want to show a video to your colleagues without using up your own storage space by all means pop it onto YouTube

- High definition camcorders are nowhere near as expensive as you think!

4 WHERE WILL PEOPLE FIND YOU?

So far we've examined how you can take a stand on what matters to you, how you can put a video onto YouTube, how to tweet or Facebook about it, displaying your photos, loads of stuff like that. We've looked at checking a bit on who your customers actually are and where they're likely to be in terms of social networking.

The bad news is that none of this matters a jot.

Let me rephrase that. Of course all of this stuff matters, but before it starts to deliver any benefit to your business or organization, people have got to know that it's there. And no matter how much you might like to kid yourself to the contrary, they won't be actively seeking you out – you need to get the message out. Your objective is presumably to increase sales and to grow your business, and whether or not you opt for social media, to fulfil that objective you need to get people to your site.

There are a number of ways of doing this. In this chapter we'll look at your website itself and how you can make it work harder in terms of optimizing it for search engines, a process (unsurprisingly) called search engine optimization (SEO). SEO can get quite technical and go under the bonnet; without meaning to gloss over that stuff, there are whole books on SEO and more SEO technology and techniques being developed every day, so for our purposes I'll stick to the basics: what you can achieve by rewording your website, why some search engines won't be able to see your website, that sort of stuff.

You can of course push your way to the top of the searches by throwing money at this activity in what used to be called advertising. In the Internet world it's termed 'pay per click' (PPC).

People do still use Internet directories, whether by searching or by working through alphabetical listings. Tragically someone forgot to give them a three-letter acronym (TLA) like SEO or PPC, so they're not as famous.

Before we look at how to make the most of what you've got, it's worth taking a step back and looking at your 'ordinary' marketing: ads in the local paper, leaflets through the door, business cards. If you want to make a load of noise by social networking, do they have the details on them that people will need? (*Note to self: Get new business cards done before book comes out or people will laugh at you.*) And conventional marketing is still relevant: Amazon is undoubtedly one of the biggest success stories on the Internet so far and when it launched in the UK in the 1990s the word-of-mouth buzz was utterly phenomenal, but what really brought it some attention were posters on the London Underground and magazine adverts.

Don't forget paper-based telephone directories. If you have a business phone number, then clearly you can go into *Yellow Pages*. This will set you on the path to appearing in the yell.com directory. Once you're there links to your details start to get distributed around the net and before you know it you're available in a number of places you didn't know were aware of you. This only works if you make your website available to them, or your email address, or your LinkedIn page – more on this stuff later.

.tel and how to use it

Hang on though, you may be saying. Am I seriously suggesting you should get a business card with your name, address, phone number, email, website, fax number, Twitter ID,

Facebook page, blog, mobile number...and chuck it all away once the Next Big Thing is in place and it's all out of date?

What I'm about to suggest is a very recent innovation and a lot of authors and commentators will tell you it hasn't stood the test of time just yet, and they'd be right. I use it, though, and it's extremely useful – it's called .tel. It looks like any other domain name – the .co.uk or .com part of your web address – but it's. tel instead. And you can't put a website on it.

This is more useful than it sounds because of what you actually can put on it, and that's a comprehensive set of contact details. I do mean comprehensive: you can add phone numbers, faxes, pagers, websites, Twitter addresses, Skype or other Internet-based phone information, SMS, instant message – and it allows you to add a few keywords so that you're not confused with someone of the same name. For example, one of the first people to hold such a domain in the UK was called Justin Hayward, who understandably put in his keywords 'not Moody Blues singer'. You can also save information privately so that only people you invite can get your home address and phone number.

There are two reasons you want all this stuff in one place. First, you can keep all of your contact details up to date and they're available to people centrally – I have mine at clapperton.tel. Second – and here's where I'm taking a bit of a flier – the people running. tel are making software available to mobile phone manufacturers, so soon you'll be able to get at .tel address entries through your address book on your phone, whether you've put them in there or not. So, if you want to know how to get in touch with me, or with the Coca-Cola

Corporation, you put the name into your address book and you get the relevant contact details, looking like any other entry in your phone book.

I'm going to take a chance and recommend buying a .tel domain, filling in the details and putting them on your business card so anyone will be able to find any of your social media contacts or other contact information at will. For the moment, include full contact details on your main website too to be safe.

SEO and other dark arts

As I've explained, search engine optimization (SEO) is the process of making your website as friendly and visible to as many search engines as you possibly can. I'll start with a disclaimer: the people who run the Internet's search engines don't disclose exactly how they work. So what I'm about to suggest you consider doing is based on educated guesswork and what's worked in the past.

The owners of Google and the other search sites (many of which feed into Google) have good reasons for keeping their exact methods a little quiet. First, it's their playground and they don't have to. Internet geeks hate it when you say that, or when Facebook or Twitter implements changes and they don't approve, but it's the reality. We don't own this stuff. Even more importantly, though, if we all knew precisely how the system worked, then the less scrupulous among us would be able to trick it, fiddle it, knacker it and generally make it useless.

Words

That said, there are ways of making whatever system there is work in your favour. The easiest part to address is what appears on your website rather than what underpins it. The first thing you check, whether you put your website together yourself or left it to a Web designer, is whether you can highlight the text by right clicking on your mouse. If you can't, then it's there as an image rather than as words. This matters, because the search engines will see it as 'some image or other' and won't add it to their lists; you need to be seen with words. Replace what you have with text; either look again at your web design program or contact your web company and get them to change it.

Keyword: words you choose to emphasise in your website, through repetition and through inclusion in areas only search engines can see.

You might now be ready to make sure your site is being indexed, but watch out. Have you written it carefully, making sure all the right keywords are prominent? Suppose you sell rivets, or consultancy. Have you got 'rivets' or 'consultancy' in your main headline, or in your standfirst? If they're not there, then the search engines can't see them. They should be prominent in the headlines, frequent in the text (and early rather than too far down); clever-clever questions in a headline just won't be understood by the search engines.

Tip!

Keyword stuffing

There is, as always, a slight complication. To catch people who try putting a wallpaper in the background of a website made up exclusively of 'rivetsrivetsrivets' or whatever, the search engines appear to be smart enough to disregard sites that go over the top and stuff in too many of a given keyword. There is presumably a cut-off point somewhere and no, they're not telling anyone where that actually comes.

There's a load of other stuff the search engines can't see at the moment (these things can change with a bit of inventiveness and the flick of a switch). Flash animation is something designers love and

Flash animation is a proprietary technology that's become commonplace on the Internet. It's a neat way of making short animations for a website, but the search engines can't see it, so be careful how you use it.

Tag: descriptive words added to a web page to help people find it when they're searching online. You can sometimes add tags to other people's pages: for example when this book was listed on Amazon prior to publication I added 'social media', 'Twitter' and other tags so that it would come up in searches people performed searches for those terms.

search engines hate, so if your landing page is an animation then you're automatically invisible to Google. If your key messages are in an animation or graphic, then once again, they're invisible to searches as they stand at the moment.

You might have noticed something by now. Search engines tend to favour straightforward sites with copy that tells you what the site's about and what it's doing, with no sophistry or undue elaboration. This is why I like the search engines' approach.

DIY software packages

There are other pieces of SEO you can slot onto your website that will help the search engines prioritize it higher than people who haven't bothered. Before we explore any of them, though, a quick check: do you know what to do with web authoring and HTML?

If not, then the chances are you'll need to use a good web designer to put your site together for you. You can get a software package that will put it together for you. Many of my own sites have been designed in Microsoft Publisher or Rapidweaver on the Mac, and they look pretty good.

There's only one problem: a colleague had a look at one of the ones in Rapidweaver to check whether it was findable by the search engines. The first thing she said was that there were no optimized tags in the <title> section at the top of the page. The title tag is one of the most important things the search engines look for when assessing my site, she said. There was also no meta description tag, which would help me control what Google said about me. The thing is, there was no way using the pre-designed template my software package was offering I would be able to put those tags and other bits of code in. So it was "objective business decision time" again: would

that make a sufficient difference to me to mean either I had to learn HTML from scratch (probably a bad option given the sophistication of other sites) or pay someone to design a new site with SEO built in at all levels? The decision will be different for each individual business.

If you don't yet have a website and are looking at using any of the inexpensive or free software on the web or at retail stores to build one, do consider that a lot of the code you'll need may be behind a door the package won't let you open. Even if it lets you copy and paste lumps of code from individual websites onto your site, the package might not let you put it in the right place.

Further SEO

Let's assume you now want to design your own website, or commission a website from a designer. If you're technically literate you'll want to think about putting in some of the elements of SEO that are invisible to the human eye and may be less obvious. Here are a few tips:

- Your domain name needs to be easy to remember so that people search for the right thing. Check to see if anyone has a similar name. A businessman in Scotland once registered—reasonably enough, as it was his name—clappertons.co.uk, compared to my clapperton.co.uk. I received a lot of email intended for him, and I know he lost some customers who thought it was unreasonable that I should politely send them on to the right place.

- Try to get the .com version of your domain name as well as .co.uk in case someone else makes an opportunistic grab at it.

- Pick a couple of keywords to optimize for each page, particularly if your business does different things. Try to pick words that

Navigation: finding your way around a website – the easier you make this on your website the better.

Sitemap: a page on your website which literally has a map of the rest of the site – a tree diagram of which pages are where.

Frames: a form of web page structure in which the page being looked at is framed by, for example, an index or navigation page which doesn't change.

don't get as many searches as the more popular variety; you'll be higher up the list when someone does do that search. For example, if you renovate vintage cars, you might do better optimizing 'vintage carburettor' than 'vintage Jaguar'; more people are likely to be looking for vintage Jags, so you'll be competing with more companies that have optimized their site for the whole brand.

- Put your preferred keywords in the <TITLE> tag.

- Use the DESCRIPTION meta tag. Meta tags are in HTML and they carry information that's read by browsers. The search engines will read and index the text in these tags and might well use that text for the description of your site that appears when someone has searched.

- Make keywords bold or italics; they'll be emphasized not only for human readers but also for search engine bots.

- No matter how sophisticated your site might be, with Java navigation and goodness knows what else, include basic HTML navigation too so that the bots can get around it and find your other pages. A sitemap also helps here.

- Try to avoid using frames on your website. If you must, remember search engines look at pages and not framesets so they won't be particularly helpful in getting your sites into the search engine results.

Exercise

You've now been reading for four chapters and I haven't set you any exercises. This will never do. For a bit of fun, please rework the following couple of paragraphs with a view to SEOing the phrase 'house cleaning'. You can see what I did with it at the end of the chapter.

An end to filth

Tired of having a dirty house? People's homes are one of the most important things in their lives and yet they apply insufficient hygiene rules to them. At Housie Housie we make sure your house is cleaner than you could have dreamed; we'll get into nooks and crannies you didn't know existed and get them clinically clean.

We've all read horror stories about salmonella, botulism and all sorts of illness caused by a basic lack of hygiene when things look clean. Call us and we'll be in to help in a jiffy.

Working with designers

Do watch those designers like the proverbial hawk. Many are excellent, but there are others who love nothing better than to put Flash animation and nothing else on your home page (the search engines won't see it), or to make your site look like their masterpiece rather than your marketing collateral. It's your property and don't let them forget it. Check your contract with them too – *you*'ve got to own the content, not them, and if you can afford to pay enough that you own the design as well, so much the better. Try not to end up like a contact of mine who fell out with his designer and hosting company and ended up unable to update his website because it was their property contractually.

Pictures

By the way, while we're on web design, a quick word about pictures; it's worth labelling them correctly. Google's picture search won't find your picture of that Aston Martin you're selling or maintaining to bring the punters in if all it can see is a label marked 'IMAGE900000324. JPG' and a blob. Interestingly, that's also all a blind person will 'see' when their screen reader tells them what's on the Web in front of them. It's worth thinking about and labelling your pictures descriptively.

Much of what people tell you about SEO makes sense until you try it. One book I read said that you should always have your domain name as the main address of a website. It is true that a few years ago, I had a note from someone about interviewing him about his professional use of the Internet for his growing business; when I noticed his company website was actually www.hiscompany.tesconet.com, I didn't take up his offer. Nevertheless, content seems to rule. I have a website at www.clapperton.co.uk. Actually that's a fib; if you type www.clapperton.co.uk into your browser you'll be forwarded to my site, which will *say* it's at clapperton.co.uk but it's actually at http://homepage.mac.com/guyclapperton/Personalpage/. Type Guy Clapperton into Google and you still find my site as the number one hit. Oddly, my colleague who had a look at my site for SEO said this would make it difficult for search engines to pick it up, but it still comes up top when you search for my name.

A quick sanity check, though: this works for me because I'm using my own name and frankly there aren't many other Guy Clappertons out there; if my name were John Smith I might be feeling differently (with apologies and due respect to any John Smiths reading this). If I were searching for myself as 'UK technology journalist' then whole bunches of them come above my listing on the results page. This is where once again it is vital to understand how your customer operates and uses the web; I know perfectly well that no editor has so few contacts they'll Google for 'UK technology journalist' so I haven't pursued it. If your customer works in a more generic way and searches for terms rather than specifically for you, you'll find it more valuable to spend some time building your business up in terms of search-friendliness.

That's enough on SEO for the moment. There's a little more about how to choose the right keywords in the next chapter where we talk specifically about blogging. For the moment, I'm ready to move on!

10Yetis Public Relations

10Yetis is a public relations organization in Gloucester. Search Google UK for 'public relations agency' and they come up top (at least they did when this book went to print). Andy Barr describes himself as 'head Yeti' – don't ask me why – and he comments that the company is competing against 84 million other sites. It achieved its position by getting links and making sure all its pictures and graphics were described properly.

'We took the time to make sure that the names we gave our images were optimized and relevant to what we do. For example, an image of a piece of coverage for a client being shown on our website was called 'public-relations-agency-client.jpg' rather than the less descriptive names people usually save images as, such as 'dave-headshot.jpg'. When it came to link building with external sites we used a combination of two key methods, the first being to speak with clients and ask them for keyword links to our site. This means that in the text '10Yetis Public Relations Agency' instead of making our name, '10Yetis', link through to our website, we asked them to make the words 'Public Relations Agency' link through to our site. The second key method of link building came from listing our work on authority news wires and again, using our target keywords as the link-through text.

'This is a slow process and you will never see overnight success. It is more about building slowly and making sure you don't take any shortcuts (such as buying external links), as Google will eventually notice and penalize your site for this. Our own internal benchmarking shows that you should slowly start to move up the rankings over a three-month period and then every time Google changes its search algorithm you can expect to rise again. It has taken us the best part of five years to get to the level we are at today, where we can introduce new keywords and rank for them fairly quickly. I would say that it took us just over a year to start ranking for competitive terms and I know from tracking where our sales enquiries come from that it has been one of the most influential areas of marketing that we have done.'

Algorithm:
mathematical formula that yields a particular result.

Pay per click (PPC)

What is good about what I've outlined above is that if you're doing it yourself it doesn't cost anything other than your time. However, if your time's more valuable to you than what you might spend on this kind of promotion, you may want to look at pay per click (PPC) advertising.

The immediate appeal of PPC is that, as the title suggests, the advertiser (that'll be you) pays only when someone clicks through to their website; if you don't get web traffic, you don't pay. The disadvantage is that like any other form of shop front, people can wander in – and you pay for their click – and then not buy anything. (If you do find a load of people are coming to your site and not engaging with you, it could be worth looking at why this might be, but that's another issue.) Another possible drawback – and only a possible one – is that PPC's not always highly regarded. As this book went to print an episode of the BBC's *Watchdog* series was aired in which a company was (of course) criticized for unfair practices; one of the things against which the *Watchdog* team reacted was that the business could be found on Google not by 'natural' search but because it had paid to reach the top slot. Sponsored and paid-for links on search engines are always labelled as such, but a section of the audience doesn't trust them and will prefer to focus on natural searches.

Natural search: search based on links and what's in the website rather than a paid for search.

The clear answer is to try to get people both ways. A combination of PPC and SEO should deliver both people who prefer to disregard the paid-for stuff and the people who'll click on the first thing they see.

Where do you start?

The basic method of setting up a PPC account is simple. You find a PPC system (we'll list some in a second), give it a credit card number and put some money into it, upload an ad, associate keywords with it and bid for these keywords. The highest bidder ought to win the highest placing, but the search engine also sanity checks your link for relevance. It guesses at this according to how many people have clicked through to your website before.

Where do I go?

At the time of writing, Google was definitely top of the tree in terms of search engines and there was no obvious competitor, in spite of new businesses offering 'semantic' searches (so you can ask a question in English rather than put in a keyword in). That method is unproven as yet. The first place to go, then, is Google and its AdWords scheme, which you'll find at www.google.co.uk/adwords.

Google believes in making everything simple for people who want to hand it money (a philosophy every business probably shares!). You go to the site, either click the 'Sign up for AdWords online' link or, if you prefer, phone the number on the site, and select which of the packages you want (if you're just beginning then the starter edition is the one to opt for). The site starts helping again: it will look for your business and see whether it can fill in the form for you and save you the bother. It asks you which country and in which area your business wants to advertise, so you can be really specific: the early days of the Internet were littered with stories of people in Tooting being approached by others in Wisconsin wanting their cars washed. You pay, you upload an image if you wish, but at the very least you get to advertise every time someone searches for your keyword; up to the level of your budget, that is.

The other ad schemes of comparable size to Google are Yahoo! and its Search Marketing scheme at searchmarketing.yahoo.com, and Microsoft's Ad centre at adcenter.microsoft.com. Yahoo! will put your ad on AltaVista, CNN, Infospace, Juno and others and Google will add your ad to AOL, Ask.com, Earthlink and others.

For my money Google is the best option because of its ubiquity, and you should also look at the same company's AdSense scheme. This is different to AdWords because it allows other sites to carry advertising; you may have seen boxes on websites with 'Advertisements by Google' on them.

Value for money

The most important thing to watch out for while you're running a PPC programme is that you're getting value for money. This is a business activity and you need to be utterly certain you're making money out of it.

Plenty of people will try to blind you with how much this sort of activity is going to be worth over the lifetime of a customer. PPC, they argue, brings the customer in once and then they keep buying, so it's worth spending £50 on getting them just the once. I'd say it isn't; if they went to Google the first time they'll do the same search again. Also, maybe getting them to follow your tweets or read your blog isn't actually going to turn all of them into long-term customers.

You ought to factor considerations like that into the price you're prepared to bid. Likewise, you need to consider the likelihood that only some of your click-through visitors will spend money, so your cost per sale is higher than your cost per click. The sooner you can work out what percentage of people actually spend money when they click through to your site, the sooner you'll know what a sensible margin is.

Never lose sight of the fact that you control the bids – and you can cap the amount you spend, so if you don't want to lose more than £150 a day then you can cap it at that rate and you're safe.

Dos and don'ts

There are good things and bad things to do with pay per click. Do remember the following:

- A click-through isn't a sale, so factor into your planning that only a certain percentage of clickers-through will spend any money.

- Remember therefore that your site has to be compelling in its own right. PPC isn't a substitute for a good web strategy, though you might be surprised how many businesses seem to think it's precisely that. Remember that if you've got a reasonable SEO strategy, the chances are that your site will be clear and relevant by default.

Finally, a few don'ts:

- Don't put PPC ads on your own site and ask people to click on them to get you a little revenue. It's against all the terms and conditions, so if you get caught you'll be turfed off the system; meanwhile, whoever you ask will start to associate you with the word 'beggar' rather than 'professional'.

- Don't buy your competitor's name as a pay per click term. Not that it's illegal, you might even get some sales out of it unless they can prove a case for passing off; but it does tell the customer that you don't have enough faith in your own capabilities and need to hijack other people's profiles. I've had it done to me and believe me, your stock doesn't go up when people find out.

- Do get an idea of what's going to exclude you from a particular site. Putting the substance of your site in an area for which the reader needs a password is bad news because Google won't see past that password so won't index your site. Also be careful not to use content to which you don't own the rights.

Directories

Loads of people still think that directories are a really neat way to search the Internet. They veer away from the randomness of a text-based search, or they reject the order in which Google is likely to place the results, and they go instead to an Internet directory.

Directories are different from search engines in a number of ways. It's useful to know a bit about these differences and I'm indebted to author of *SEO For Dummies*, Peter Kent. He points out:

- The directories don't send bots out to sites to inspect them, although they may want to check your site is still there.

- Directories don't read and store your information. (See how Google results give you the first couple of lines of text on a website it finds? A directory won't, simple as that.)

- The contents of your website are therefore not going to make a scrap of difference to the directories.

- You can't submit individual web pages to directories, only complete websites.

Kent points to the Yahoo! directory as one of the most important. You can see it at http://dir.Yahoo.com. By now you're wondering why both he and I think it's important if you need me to tell you where to find it, and I can see the point. The thing is, it feeds into Yahoo!'s search engine, and as you'll appreciate, that is indeed important. Likewise, the Open Directory Project (www.dmoz.org) feeds into Google's directory and hence its search engine. Everything's interlinked.

You might not want to use a directory. You might not think your customers want to use a directory. But if you're listed there it's another point the search engines will consider in your favour when they're ranking your site against others.

Submission

The really bad news is that you have to submit to most directories manually. There honestly isn't a simple automatic way of doing it. Ignore the spammers who email you and tell you they can do it automagically for only $100 or whatever, they'll be offering to flog you Viagra this time next week and it'll never arrive.

The worse news is that to get listed on Yahoo! costs a fair bit – $300–600 per annum. But once again, look at what it's going to do for your business. If it isn't going to pay for itself you don't want to do it, simple as that. If you still think it's worth the cost, read on.

First, a little sanity check. Go to http://dir.yahoo.com and search for your company name. You might find you're already in the directory. If not, do a little check; tick 'the Web' at the top and search the Internet instead. Note that my own website didn't come up in the directory at all but was still no. 1 when I searched the Internet for Guy Clapperton. This will be a help to know if your business has an unusual name; I'm not in competition with that many Guy Clappertons, so my absence from the directory doesn't bother me. If you're a carpenter and want people to find you, it might be different.

Go to the Yahoo! Directory main page, browse the categories and find the best match for your site. There's a box in every category marked

'Suggest a site';enter your site, follow the instructions on screen and be ready with a credit or debit card. You can put your business into several categories and pay for the privilege each time.

The Open Directory is free, which sounds better. It doesn't guarantee a listing after you've submitted, though. Submission is easy: go to www.dmoz.org, find a category, pick 'Suggest URL' and follow the instructions. Your page will be examined eventually by one of 8,000 editors managing 70,000 categories. It will take time. They're human and they admit they lose entries sometimes.

There are also second-tier players, the smaller people in the directory market. There are literally hundreds of them and I'm not about to start listing them, as loads of them come and go all the time. Remember also that many of these take a feed from Yahoo! and the Open Directory.

Local directories

So far I've been talking about the global directories, and by now you'll have seen the deliberate mistake in the previous section. I suggested you might be a carpenter, and you might want to be listed so that people can find you more easily when they search the web.

Well, there's no reason why not. But if you have a particularly web-savvy set of customers, they might be looking in the local directories instead. Have a look at Qype; it's a series of directories by area and people like hairdressers not only get listed, they get reviewed. Your business might be better suited to a paid-for listing in there. Finding them is easy: search for (yourtown) directory and see what comes up. Remember to look before you leap: if you run a restaurant, for example, be prepared to get bad reviews as well as good ones if your local directory runs reviews. It can still work in your favour as long as the good outweigh the bad.

However, do not try to scam the system by writing your own reviews. One of my favourite TV programmes is *Gordon Ramsay's Kitchen Nightmares*, in which the chef rescues ailing restaurants. In one of the British episodes he found an online review of a particularly poor restaurant that said it was better than either his or Jamie Oliver's eateries. He asked the owner whether he'd written the review himself. The owner denied it twice then eventually broke down and confessed; he'd been desperate for customers so he'd invented the review. It didn't get him customers. It got him humiliation on national television. Be warned!

Business directories

There are also a number of directories specifically designed for the business user. In the UK, one of the main ones is BT Tradespace (www.bttradespace.com). You don't need to be a BT customer to get into this and the basic 'shop front' is free. Go to the link on the right of the page, sign up and decide which category you need to get into. You're allowed to upload podcasts and videos free of charge.

Podcast: an audio programme you can download from the Internet.

Also check out Ziki (www.ziki.com), whose blog said it was being rethought as we went to print. Simply go to the site and click the link to register on the right; like a Google Ad, you won't be charged unless someone actually logs on to your site.

When in doubt, cheat

OK, cheating's not quite what I'm about to suggest. But you might find a listing on someone else's website will do very well for pushing you into a search listing. By now you'll have gathered that I'm overly fond of searching for my own name on Google to make sure I'm in the right place and that nobody else is ranking above me. So I enter Guy Clapperton, my website comes up and, four places down, my LinkedIn profile is listed too.

That's right. Social networking site LinkedIn is putting my name out there and doing a bit of the SEO and directory placement for me. I search for our local Indian takeaway, which doesn't have its own website, and guess what: it comes up, but under the VirtualNorwood local directory and I'm taken straight to its entry. Your BT Tradespace or Ziki entry will work for you in a similar way.

So, you want to be found but you're not sure you want to go to the trouble of putting a full-blown website together? That's no problem. Social media is the way!

The semantic web

As this book went to print a new form of directory was emerging, called the semantic web. The first sign of this was a search engine – the company behind it hates that term but I'll use it – called Wolfram Alpha. This could throw a lot of the rules of searching out of the window, but don't write everything else off just yet.

The idea is that existing search engines don't work as they ought to. If you came to me in person and asked for a good restaurant near Crystal Palace, where I live, and instead of recommending somewhere I sent you to some sort of listings page, I'd appear rude. If you asked me what was on at the local cinema and instead of telling you I gave you a web reference, you'd also consider me impolite. It's different if you're talking to a computer, naturally enough. Google gives you a list of websites that might help you, based on keywords you've put into the search engine, and we all find it perfectly normal.

That, say the semantic web people, isn't good enough. What if there were a website (and it's been tried with AskJeeves.co.uk) which allowed you to enter a question in English – say, what's the weather like in Manchester? – and it gave you the information straight away? That's what Wolfram Alpha does. At least, it does with that question. In other cases it's less straightforward. I tried – on day one – entering my own name to see what it came up with. Google came out with my own website, numerous sites on which my articles and journalism appear and even a book of short stories to which I'd forgotten I'd contributed in the mid-1990s. Wolfram Alpha told me it wasn't sure what to do with my query.

This might mean a number of things. It could mean the new search engines have an egomaniac detector, but I doubt it. It could mean that the one I tried was very American-centric, a criticism it has certainly faced; I tried entering Paul McCartney's name and it gave me his birthday and age but no more, which suggests it was underpopulated with information early on.

The jury, in other words, remains out on this new form of searching. Certainly Google had announced a substantial redesign as we went to print and was aiming to start behaving in a similar way, or at least attach more importance to different media like video and photography. The rules about how to get to the top of these piles – if indeed Wolfram Alpha doesn't do away with these piles of pages completely – are continually being rewritten.

Action points

Thinking matter

1. What are the key things you want to sell, and what words are associated with these when people search?

2. Is your website clearly written or is it a 'personality' site? These are often problematic for search!

3. Can you try formulating a few sentences with SEO in mind?

Do list

• Check what comes up when you search for your sort of business on Google and note what the companies you find there are doing in their SEO activities.

• Get rid of anything but readable text and simple pictures on the first page of your website.

And finally: the exercise

Hopefully you had a go at the exercise I set earlier in this chapter in which you rewrote a few lines and SEOd them for the phrase 'house cleaning'. Here they are again to save you turning back:

An end to filth

Tired of having a dirty house? People's homes are one of the most important things in their lives and yet they apply insufficient hygiene rules to them. At Housie Housie we make sure your house is cleaner than you could have dreamed; we'll get into nooks and crannies you didn't know existed and get them clinically clean.

We've all read horror stories about salmonella, botulism and all sorts of illness caused by a basic lack of hygiene when things look clean. Call us and we'll be in to help in a jiffy.

OK, problem number one is that the phrase 'house cleaning' doesn't occur at all. The only correct answer was therefore to rewrite and restructure the whole lot. The header should have the phrase in it somewhere too. You might try:

House cleaning gets serious

House cleaning is something that concerns everyone, but not everyone has the knowledge they need. Housie Housie takes house cleaning very seriously, fighting hygiene threats and defending the place in which you live.

We get at the nooks and crannies standard equipment can't reach and get your house clinically clean. Housie Housie: house cleaning by professionals.

OK, I calmed it down a bit and took out some of the hype. But what's important is that the second version, even though it's less in-your-face aggressive, would work better in a search.

5 THE JOY OF TEXT

Yes, I know, every time someone wants to write about writing words they come out with that hokey old 'The joy of text' heading. I've been doing it since 1989; what can I tell you, I'm juvenile.

In this chapter we're going to park the bells and whistles, the video, the multimedia. We're going to look at things you can do with text only – the really, really simple stuff – and how to use it to engage with people. We're going to look not only at the technical side of getting a blog online but also at populating it with interesting and engaging content.

Why do you blog?

Blogging itself is simple, but this book isn't just about the physical act of doing things online. Before you put finger to keyboard you need to consider: why blog? What is it about your business that is going to give you something to say today, tomorrow, next week? (Hint: make it engaging and interesting. Glad we got that straight.)

Also you need to be a bit ruthless with yourself. Are you, or have you ever been, a good writer? Really? Good, then there's no problem. Or if you're less than confident, then maybe one of your team is excellent at it. Someone has to be. You don't want misunderstandings, you don't want an online row breaking out – you want an engaged community of users who'll go out and act as ambassadors for your brand.

It's important, then, to start with your desired outcome; that's a theme I hope you'll be picking up throughout this book. Your outcome might be more customers, or it might be more purchases from your existing customers.

If it's the latter, the first thing you do is...ask some customers. Do they read blogs? Are they interested in the sort of thing you're likely to have to say to them on your blog? If not, you might be well advised to forget it. You can also forget it if you haven't anything interesting to say.

Many of the bad blogs I've seen suffer from a number of things:

- Insufficiently riveting content – and this means in week 50 as well as week 1. So many of them run out of steam.

- Inability to write well. I'm a journalist and author, so my professional discipline is going to lead me to be critical of any mistake someone makes in terms of grammar, spelling or punctuation, but a basic error is going to look bad to anyone else too. So watch it. No apostrophes for plurals, no their/there muck-ups and make sure what you write makes sense.

- Spam in the comment section – so it looks as though nobody's keeping an eye on it.

If you're after new customers then blogging can be even more tricky. You have to write something worth reading of course, but you also have to write it in such a way that the search engines will find it.

That said, let's step back and look at the basic principles of blogging. A blog can be many things depending on who's writing it; the blogger, in webspeak. Essentially it's a collection of thoughts, pictures and links someone wants to share with the outside world. Some reasons people use blogs include:

- To extend their journalism: even senior journalists like Robert Peston and Nick Robinson at the BBC, and Jon Snow at Channel

4 News, have their blogs online to inform people of what's happening and to fill in a little more background depth than is possible in a broadcast.

- To air their thoughts: several business and technology analysts use blogs to bypass the journalism 'filter' that might dilute or interpret their comments in a way they don't want. Look also at the box on Alex Bellinger's Smallbizpod, in which podcasting and blogging are his chief means of communication.

- Brand extension: look at Innocent Drinks (http://innocentdrinks.typepad.com). There's a lot about product but it's done in an entertaining, 'we don't take ourselves too seriously' manner that reiterates and expands on the brand's values.

I'm excluding any personal reasons someone might have for launching a blog. This is a business book, after all. Let's assume, then, that you've decided blogging is for you, you have something to say and you're ready to start.

Smallbizpod

Alex Bellinger, director of Smallbizpod, started blogging early on. 'SmallBizPod launched in March 2005 on Blogger and was very much an experiment focused on podcasts with entrepreneurs,' he explains. 'Being the first business podcast in the UK helped get the word out, as did traditional PR and the online networking, which formed an intrinsic part of blogging and podcasting from the outset.

'There was a great sense of camaraderie among bloggers and podcasters, particularly in the early days. We all helped each other spread the word about what was going on, primarily through online conversations and commenting that blogging helped facilitate.'

Clearly, this changed over time and by now blogging and podcasting are as competitive as any other area of business, but Bellinger believes it's still essential for a business as long as the content is compelling. 'These platforms give anyone with something interesting to say the freedom to do so, but more importantly the freedom to scale their online presence,' he says. 'The fact that SmallBizPod can run on the same platform as Techcrunch, or Le Monde, or the New York Times and for virtually zero cost is amazing.

'To put it bluntly, without blogging, SmallBizPod as a business wouldn't exist.'

How do you blog?

Blogging is really simple once you have the right software, either on your computer or, as is increasingly common, on the web. First, I want to consider solutions that allow you to develop a whole website, rather than just a blog.

Apple's iLife has its own iWeb software, which has a blogging template on it, there are many alternatives such as Sandvox and I use Rapidweaver from Realmac. I'm not going to recommend an individual piece of software to you since preferences are very individual. Instead, I'll talk you through some of the more common options and issues to consider, and refer to some of the packages I've used (and which are still current – I'm still fond of Microsoft Publisher 97 because of the simplicity but it's no longer available).

iWeb has a number of advantages, not least that it's part of the set of software that comes with many Macs, so it's inexpensive. It offers a number of pre-designed templates; you pick the design and the colour scheme and then add whichever pages your site needs. These include photo pages, pages for movies, pages for a podcast and of course a blog (you can embed your video on your own page and upload it to the Internet intact, but I wouldn't bother as long as YouTube is offering to handle the bandwidth and distribution issues free of charge). There is sample text and photography on all of the blog templates; simply highlight the text and type over it, and drag and drop a replacement picture. It's as easy as that.

RapidWeaver works in a similar way: choose a template and add a blog page. Adding blog entries is easy by hitting the 'plus' button on the blog page and then uploading the site to your webspace. RapidWeaver has the advantage of showing you the HTML code, so if you haven't got the right tags in place for SEO purposes you can see that. Unfortunately you can't edit the raw code, but you can put a piece of code into the page and hope it lands in the right place (there would be a good chance of really screwing the page up if they let everyone loose on the raw code).

PC users are far from left out. Have a look at Microsoft's website at http://windowslivewriter.spaces.live.com/blog/cns!D85741BB5E0BE8AA!174.entry – you can download LiveWriter software from there as long as you have Windows 2000 or something more recent, and start designing and updating web pages from the minute you've installed the software. This includes the ability to blog and is aimed at people who don't have the time or inclination to manage their own web space. Microsoft will host the pages for you as well as provide the tools to design them.

An even more comprehensive package is Serif's WebPlus X2, which comes with a book that starts you thinking properly about web design. It's all too easy to allow a website to grow in an unmanaged way, so Serif recommends you start with a tree diagram telling you where things are going to go, what's a subpage of what and so on. It's a methodical way of putting the pages together.

There is a third way of compiling a website, which is to assemble it all online. This differs from, say, Blogger or Wordpress, which also offer the online assembly of a blog, in that you can put together a complete website rather than just the blog bit. Go to www.moonfruit.com, a UK company that has an online site designer: you choose your template, add the text and it's online all but immediately. The paid-for account even builds in ecommerce through PayPal. Look also at Mr Site's Takeaway Website Pro; this comes either on the web or as packaged software, but the CD that comes in the box is the manual only. The software offers a lot of ecommerce features, including stock control and up to 99 items per page if you're selling stuff online, as well as a PayPal shop, and it'll match your business cards and stationery to the design of your site. It'll even take care of a lot of the SEO issues for you.

There are many ways of getting a blog and a site online and some will suit you better than others. It's worth having a play with them before you start to publicize where people can find you on the web, so that when you do announce it it's permanent.

PayPal is a way of paying for items online using your credit card, where the merchant simply registers with PayPal rather than with a bank. In this way as a business you can be taking payments online within minutes rather than months of deciding to make your service or goods available online.

Remember:

- A web-savvy person will recognize a site designed on a template from one of the packages I've described. This may or may not matter to you.

- The automatic upload that these pieces of software offer is splendid – until it falls over and you have no way of uploading your site. This has happened to me.

- Many of these web design programs have their own bits of stray code attached, so that the software gets a credit deep within your site, for example. This can make transferring your site to another piece of software quite tricky!

- On the other hand, there is probably no quicker way for a novice to get a good-looking and functional website up within a few hours.

Hosted or self-hosted?

One thing you need to decide is whether you want to host your own blog or opt for one of the free and easy options. The latter are good because they are (a) free and (b) easy. The former offers you some more flexibility: you can't, for example, put an external advertisement on anything hosted by Wordpress, but you can use the company's software to make a blog and, as long as it's on your own server, you can put what you want on it.

Take the Wordpress system. Wordpress.com is great at first glance (and depending on your objective it might be all you need). You go to the website, set up an account, add a blog entry, hit 'Publish' and it's done. Could anything be better? Well, maybe not better, but take a look at Blogger as well. The screens look very different indeed but the functions are much the same.

Your domain

You might want to get your blog registered with a memorable domain. Most registration companies will allow you to point your domain at someone else's servers. So if you registered something with 1–2–3-Reg, Easily.net or any of the others, you could have it pointing to your webspace, to someone else's webspace, anywhere.

For example, maybe you decide to get a bang up-to-date view of my social networking blog. You enter www.socialnetworkingblog.co.uk in your browser and as far as you're concerned it's got there. Except it hasn't. It's actually gone to Easily.co.uk, which manages the domain for me. Until April 2009 Easily pointed people at guyclapperton.wordpress.com, where they'd see the rather ornate blog I was running at the time. I realized pretty quickly that Wordpress wasn't going to allow advertising – which, as a self-employed person in a recession, probably mattered to me more than it would matter to many readers – so I opted to host it myself. Rather than book some more webspace I used some I already had; www.socialnetworkingblog.co.uk now points to http://homepage.mac.com/guyclapperton/Personalpage/Socialnetworkingblog/Socialnetworkingblog.html if you please: really simple for you to type in the original, really easy for me to update on Apple's website. I can of course move it again any time I want, and because www.clapperton.co.uk points to the Mac page as well I can point people to the blog from my main site.

There are disadvantages too, however. The new site is nowhere near as easy to track as the old one – finding how many people have visited takes actual work. It was more important to me to try and make a little income out of it; you have to decide what works for you.

As with everything to do with social networks, you look at the business case and then decide.

Also be aware of how many permutations there might be of your blog's name. It can cost a fortune if you're registering yourblog.co.uk, yourblog.com, yourblog.net and all the rest. It's up to you how far you go with this. But never forget that if you're successful, someone will try to attract your web traffic away from you and they might well do it dishonestly: they might register a misspelt version of your name so bad spellers end up on their site, or they might look for a region in which you don't own your company's name. How far you go in protecting yourself is up to you.

Your online identity

It's here that we have to look not so much as what you want to achieve by going online – that's relatively easy and you'll probably have had an objective in mind before you picked this book up – as what your online presence is going to say about your company.

A while ago I was speaking at an event at which social media types were raising a number of issues. One of them asked whether when tweeting, blogging, Facebooking and the rest she should be 'herself', or whether she'd be better off acting as company spokesperson only.

This isn't as simple to answer as you might think. On the one hand, if you're acting on behalf of an organization you might want to consider being pretty straight about that. But who's going to read company posts only? Holding people's interest on, say, Twitter or your blog can be really tricky if you're only going to make company announcements. On the other hand, if you're too personal about things then you start to affect the company's image because you're so well known as part of the organization; it becomes your business, not you, that's associated with 'hangover every morning'. That's an extreme example, but it's worth considering: are you in danger of associating your personal traits too much with your business?

Let's look at this from the other side. A short while ago someone on Twitter put a note up asking PR people not to send press releases to his work email address because they weren't relevant – he was a blogger, he said, not a journalist, so press releases weren't relevant anyway. I won't enter the debate about bloggers becoming journalists; the issue here was that he perceived his work email as entirely separate from his social networking email, and this was presumably different again from his personal email. Many people will be familiar with the idea of a separate email for work and personal use, much as they are with phone numbers; social networks add a different dimension. It's worth considering just how personal you want your tweets in particular to appear. Try following @whatleydude for an idea of how it's done really well: until he left in August 09 he was known to be part of Spinvox and represented the brand well whilst retaining his personal voice.

You could try following me as @guyclapperton – but remember that the rules are slightly different for freelances, in that we are literally our own business, so we don't have to take anyone else's views or sensibilities into account.

SEO for blogs

In the last chapter we started talking about search engine optimization (SEO). This is how you maximize the text on your website – including that on your blog – to make sure it gets picked up by the search engines.

As I said there, the search engines don't actually tell anyone how they pick the websites up and select them. What we do know is that Google uses some of the following criteria:

- How many sites are linking to yours and how old they are. I registered www.clapperton.co.uk in the mid-1990s, so when I set up my media training site at www.mediatrainer.biz and linked to it, the search engines picked that up as 'likely to be legit' pretty quickly. Starting up in isolation is more difficult.

- Tags: these are little subject headers you can add in separately from your message. Make them relevant!

- Keywords: your site will be searched for important words to make sure they appear in the right places. Make keywords you think will be searched for prominent in the headline and the body text, and don't worry too much about a little repetition (although if it gets silly the search engines will ignore you, and nobody's saying where exactly the dividing line is).

If all that sounds a little intimidating then don't forget, it's basically the same sort of marketing writing technique you'll have been using already: targeted, succinct, and with the right keywords.

There's a trick question in there waiting to be sprung. Many people assume they 'know' what sort of keywords their customers will look for on the Internet. Some of them may even be right, but here's an experiment: go to https://adwords.google.co.uk/select/KeywordToolExternal (if they've changed it don't worry, do a Google search for Google Ads Keyword Tool), then put in the keyword you think your customers will search for. Enter the text it asks for as well and hit 'Enter' – you'll get not only information on how many people are searching for the keyword you asked for, but keywords like it. For example, I worked quite hard to make sure people searching for 'media trainer' would find me. Only when I checked the Google Adwords facility did I find that in the previous month 170 people had searched for 'media trainer' while 12,100 searched for 'media training'. You can imagine that elements of my site were rewritten pretty quickly after that!

As for a website, you need to check that your software posts entries as text rather than images or anything else the search engines won't be able to see. Too many graphics, loads of animation and your message will be drowned out.

If you can bear all the above in mind for your blog, which might change as often as daily, then you should start to see traffic pick up on your site.

Traffic is the number of people who come to your website.

Customer comments

Monitor your blog regularly. One of the lessons you'll learn very early on is that not all of your customers are interested in commenting and making your blog engaging, but some of them may be a little too voluble for your liking. A magazine found this – no names, no pack drill – it invited readers to comment on their articles (not quite a blog but similar) and found the same two commentators making exactly the same nihilistic comments to everything. Nobody else bothered. It's up to you to stimulate the debate.

Likewise, when I first started running my small business website in the 1990s I tried asking questions to promote a response. I was pretty disheartened when nobody answered – and believe me, nothing looks more ridiculous on your website than a solicitation for a conversation in which it's obvious from the silence that nobody wants to take part. Again, it's up to you to do something about it, but above all to read your customers and prospects right in the first place.

Oh, and do have a look at the legal note in the box.

Warning: libel

If someone says something libellous and it's on your blog, the person or body being libelled may have no option but to sue you as well as the writer. That's right: it's on your blog, it's your property.

There are a few case histories you can follow on this, the most obvious being Godfrey v. Demon Internet (1999). To cut a long story short (if you want more detail there's plenty on Google), the plaintiff in the case (Prof. Godfrey) found that someone had sent a message that appeared to be from him (but wasn't) to an Internet newsgroup. He faxed his ISP, Demon Internet, which didn't remove the post and he considered it defamatory to his reputation. The judge in the case decided that in this instance the ISP was acting as a publisher and was therefore voluntarily publishing something it knew to be defamatory, so it lost the case.

There are more recent examples. In 2007 self-published author Christopher Carrie put up a blog that was critical of many elements of the life of *Lord of the Rings* author JRR Tolkien. Tolkien's family put up a spirited defence on the blog and made counter-allegations against Carrie – I won't bore you with the details, again they're around on the web it you want. The point was that Carrie, alarmed at what the Tolkiens were saying, sued them and the judge decided – I'd suggest reasonably enough – that if Carrie could have zapped the comments from his blog really easily then he, not the Tolkiens, was responsible for the allegations remaining there for as much as a minute after he'd seen them.

This makes you responsible for quite a lot on your blog, particularly if you're hosting your own. A few years ago I wrote a blog for a media company in Brighton, Mousetrap Media. The idea was to have a journalist commentating on developments in the press and media and it got a fair bit of pick-up. Then it got hit by the spam-bots. I hadn't been looking at the comments carefully as I was writing for someone else, but when one of my readers sent a mail asking whether I *really* approved of the gambling and sexual sites my blog appeared to be offering, I got down to removing all those comments by hand (OK, I told the bloke in Brighton to do it, and he did so at great length and in his own time). It wasn't just moral outrage, although the idea that my blog was being hijacked for that sort of pursuit wasn't pleasant. It was partly because I realized that immediately I was aware of those comments and come-ons on my blog, I could be blamed for their presence. I have no idea how that one would have turned out in court, nor did I feel much like testing the idea.

Essentially, if it's on your blog, you own it and are responsible for it. This means not only offering value to your customers and prospects, but taking responsibility for anything anyone else puts up there, whether they are colleagues, customers, spammers, competitors or simple troublemakers. Don't be put off – a few minutes a day might well take care of this – but build it into your business plan.

Twitter

It's worth looking at Twitter again in this chapter. Twitter is probably the de facto text-only social network, even if it does carry a picture of the sender next to each message. As we established in Chapter 3, a tweet is 140 characters including spaces, but there are a few things it's not and yet people still treat it this way:

- It's not an open invitation to tell everyone what you had for breakfast.

- Private conversations carried out in response to a message can be constructive as long as you don't exclude other people; take it to direct messages if you want to go really private, or take it to email, phone, visits, it doesn't have to be on Twitter!

- At the same time, everything doesn't have to be about selling – your value on Twitter is more than just as a sales pitch merchant.

It can be worth rereading the section on your online identity in relation to what you do on Twitter. It's not an easy concept and it needs to be dealt with.

Action points

Thinking matter

1. Does your product or service lend itself to updates?

2. Can you or a colleague sustain a blog or Twitter feed over a long period of time?

3. Can you say more than just add updates to your self-promotion all the time?

Do list

- Register a domain name that's meaningful to your company.

- Look at Blogger.com and Wordpress, and decide whether to opt for a hosted or self-hosted blog.

- Get blogging!

6 WHY DON'T WE DO IT ON THE ROAD?

Cloud computing: computing in which your computer acts as a terminal and you're using a computer elsewhere. It's not all that extraordinary – there are many complex applications but a simple Hotmail account is an example of cloud computing.

You're sold on social networking, or at least you've decided it's going to do something for your business. Then you start to think, if only it could do something for you when you're away from your desk.

Social media is by no means restricted to your computer when you're sitting at your desk. Mobile working has exploded unbelievably over the last few years through a few technologies: first laptops, then mobile phones, then smartphones, then cloud computing. That's a gross simplification, but it's most of what you need to know. Let's put it this way: I'm writing the opening paragraphs to this chapter in a sport club while my daughter has her tennis lesson. I'm working on my laptop, but I'm actually logged into Google Apps, using the word processor Google offers free of charge. The advantage is that if the battery runs down and I have to continue it on my phone, I can do it.

The same principle that allows Google to 'host' my book – in other words it's on their computers, wherever they are, whereas it feels as though I'm typing it on my laptop – is allowing me to tweet at the same time. I'm logged in to Twitter using the Tweetdeck program. The fact that other people's tweets are on another computer somewhere, downloading to me, is incidental.

Google Apps is a selection of web-based applications that Google offers customers, competing with Microsoft Office and the like.

If you're logging on to something remotely (and in the case of social media that's what you're doing: Facebook, Twitter and all the rest aren't installed on your computer, they're somewhere else and you're logged onto them), there's no need to be at a desktop computer. You can be just about anywhere.

In this chapter I'll run through the basics of what you can do with a few applications on your mobile phone. I'll look at what sort of phone you need. I won't discuss using social media on a laptop, because that's just using a smaller computer and as long as you have a decent Internet connection the process should be exactly the same.

Phones and smartphones

A while ago there was an ad campaign urging people to upgrade their phones because an old one looks embarrassing. Nobody should respond to that sort of ad; if your phone works and you're happy with it don't even think of upgrading it. If you want to use it for social networking, though, the situation's a little different. You'll need something with a decent-sized screen and the ability to input text with more than a numeric keypad if you're going to do it properly.

You're looking, in fact, for a smartphone. We'll talk about the models in a second, but first a word about costs – they cost quite a lot. If you want one that's unlocked – in other words, neither tied to a contract nor shackled to any particular phone network – you can expect to pay upwards of £300. If you're not sure you're going to make up the difference in your business plan then you know the routine: don't do it.

So, a little look at some of the hardware on offer. This isn't going to be exhaustive, as the models of phone available tend to change every 18 months or so. Much of the substance will be the same, however.

Apple iPhone

The fashion statement of choice and for many people the ideal midpoint between a music machine and a phone. If you want something that's going to fit into your corporate network then you might as well forget it now; although it can be done, the Blackberry is much better suited to straight business than the iPhone.

The current model is the iPhone 3G S, which offers connections to the fast 3G data network. In the UK it's available either on pre-pay or at a vastly reduced price on contract from O2, Carphone Warehouse with others due to start selling it in late 2009/early 2010. The model name and the exclusivity can change, and the operating system is bound to be upgraded sooner or later, but the basics of the phone won't alter.

There are many add-ons and bits of software called 'apps' (short for applications) for the iPhone. You get them by visiting the iTunes store on your computer or phone, searching for the app you want and downloading it to your phone. If you download it to your computer it'll be on the phone next time you synchronize. It's really that simple.

Many of the social networks have their own iPhone apps. Go to the iTunes store and search for LinkedIn, Facebook or MySpace and you'll find free apps you can download for all of them. Enter your account details when you're on a WiFi or 3G network and you'll be able to do everything on your phone that you could do with your computer.

Twitter is a little different, because there are many different apps for accepting and managing your tweets. People are developing apps all the time, but at the moment some of the better ones are:

● Twitterfon: download this and it will separate your tweets into general tweets from your friends, direct messages and replies/mentions. There is a free version that carries an advert or for a small amount of money you can have an ad-free version.

● Twittelator: a paid-for app, this does a lot more than the rest. Of course it handles the basics, but when you press the picture you get a very clear set of options including reply, private message, retweet, email the tweet, copy the tweet, copy a link to the tweet. If you're likely to want to share things then you need this sort of

I'd love to give you a simple web address for Apple's iTunes store but I can't; it's actually built into the iTunes music management program. If you want to get at it, download iTunes (it's free) from Apple. com/uk and then click on the iTunes Store sign on the left-hand side of iTunes. I wouldn't bother if you're not using an iPod or iPhone.

flexibility, even if it does cost nearly £3 (don't sniff, that's expensive for an iPhone app).

- Aggregators: if you decide you need Facebook, Twitter and the others in your hand when you're out, then you may want to look at one of the aggregator apps that put all of these into one. Go to the Apple store and check Nimbuzz, which will find all your Windows Live Messenger, Skype, Google Talk, Facebook, Yahoo!, MobileMe and MySpace contacts and a load of others. Bafflingly, it doesn't work with Twitter; presumably they're working on that. Yahoo! has also issued an aggregator app that takes in Twitter, Facebook, Bebo, Dopplr, Flickr, Friendster, Last.FM, MySpace, YouTube and several different emails.

People are coming out with different apps all the time, so do check the iTunes store to see what's available.

Google Android

In 2007 Google started making noises about launching its own mobile phone environment. The first phones to use it (the system was called Android but the phones weren't; technology companies are helpful like that) came out from T-Mobile in the UK the following year. Called the G1, the next version, which might if we're very lucky be called the G2 but don't bet on it, was due sometime in 2009.

Google's Android environment shares many features with Apple's iPhone, except that the aim of the Google phone is to get you online and looking at Google's various sites as often as possible. Like Apple it has opened itself up to developers, so if you buy one of these phones you can get a Facebook application called fBook (effectively a wrapper for the Internet site), a Facebook application in the shape of Twindroid or eBuddy; no doubt there will be many more as the phones continue to grow.

Windows Mobile

Many Windows applications have their mobile equivalents for Windows-based mobile phones, including some of the snazzier offerings from Samsung. CeTwit and Tiny Twitter will keep you on Twitter for as long as you like, while Friendmobilizer will allow you to keep track of Facebook.

Symbian

The other major form of mobile phone is based on the Symbian operating system, favoured by Nokia, Sony Ericsson and others. Facebook, Twitter, MySpace and other applications are being released to work on those phones as well.

The gotchas

The applications available for all of these phones vary from day to day as people develop different things and make them available – and seriously, the range grows every day.

However, things to watch for include:

- Data charges: if you're away from a usable WiFi hotspot and start to use a 3G network, you might well find that you're incurring a lot of costs. If you're travelling abroad and continue to use data as well as voice, the price could go up dramatically. It's never easy to tell just how much data you're using, I certainly don't know what a gigabyte looks like. If you can be a bit sparing with your use of the mobile Internet, do so.

- Speed: most of these applications will work very well indeed on a 3G network. Unfortunately if you move away from this network, say you're on a coach, the speed can slow right down and keep you waiting a long time to receive even the smallest message on Facebook.

Why use mobile social media?

Now you know how it's done, you need to know why you'd bother. Frankly, any fool can waste time checking blogs and all sorts of stuff on a train, but some people prefer to have their downtime to themselves.

Peter Linton

Peter Linton has been in public relations for over 20 years. His current role is as PR coordinator for computer peripheral manufacturer Logitech, and as such he has to keep in touch with many journalists who specialize in writing about technology. 'I read Twitter most days on my half-hour each way commute on the train on m.twitter.com (Windows Mobile smartphone, Opera browser),' he explains. 'It's a great way to keep in touch with what my press contacts are up to, mostly on a personal level.' He also follows a couple of key publications for news input, and takes account of the fact that he is getting a snapshot of what's happening at any particular time and will miss stuff. 'As for output, our press announcements are time sensitive, so if I am on the road/rails when we are making an announcement I will tweet the headline and a link from my phone,' he adds. 'Otherwise Tweetdeck from my PC. Our agency will often retweet my tweets – they have more contacts than I do.'

This sounds pretty basic and of course it is. Linton's job is to contact as many journalists as possible to spread the word about each device, and he sees himself as obliged to use as many touch points as he can. He eschews the 'I've just had a coffee' school of Twittering. Almost subconsciously, he's also evaluated his audience and its potential for receiving information in this way; tech specialist journalists should certainly be comfortable in front of a computer screen or mobile device for following his tweets, and they have a vested interest in knowing what his company's up to. His Twitter activity is therefore measured and he has a good reason – time sensitivity – for ensuring a mobile presence.

Many people use social media online to keep themselves more up-to-date than they would otherwise be. Media consultant Mark Crosby explains, 'As a PR consultant I'm constantly keeping track of customers, breaking news, stories and interesting articles. Through Twitter I have a resource that can give me live updates on all of these, acting like an interactive RSS feed.

'I use a range of Twitter clients on my iPhone, but mostly Twitterfon, because it gives me full use of Twitter while on the move, allowing me to retweet, post pictures, follow links and most importantly to interact.

'Since joining Twitter about 12 months ago I have been able to connect with journalists in a way that suits them and also see when businesses are searching for the services that I offer. Through using Twitter on a mobile I am able to stay on top of these opportunities while away from the office.

'While there is an argument that I could wait until I get back to the office, a key point of social media websites, like Twitter, is that they're constantly updating and due to the high volume of traffic on the site, by the time I return to the office I could have missed an opportunity that someone else has picked up on. As a result of using Twitter on my mobile I have picked up new customers, interacted with journalists and been able to seize opportunities to fit their deadlines.

'Media and social media move at such a pace that being able to access the information on Twitter while away from a computer is essential to anybody working in these circles.'

Like any mobile computing application, mobile social networking turns otherwise useless time – travelling on a train, waiting for a bus, just about anything – into productive time. It also means that if an opportunity for customer care or proactive selling comes up online, you don't miss it.

The media isn't the only sector that can look at mobile social media usefully, of course. Any self-employed person who is out of the office for any length of time can use mobile social networking to keep tabs on what colleagues and competitors are doing at any point. I've found it useful as a marketing tool: I mention what I'm doing online and people commission me for more because I've reminded them I'm around, possibly on their own mobile device!

Audible social media

It's also worth looking at what you can add to your blog, a tweet or a Facebook page in terms of audio content. There are two primary pieces of technology that will help you do this. One is called Audioboo, which is becoming well known and as long as you use an iPhone it's ideal. If you don't use an iPhone, you can't use it, it's not for you.

To start using Audioboo you need to do two things. First, go to www.audioboo.fm – the site keeps apologizing for looking scrappy but it'll do for your purposes. Along the top there's a box with 'Don't have an account? Sign up now' written on it. Click on that, they only need very basic details and you'll find you have an Audioboo account. Remember your sign-up and password, these are important.

Next, either on your iPhone or your computer, visit the iTunes store, search for Audioboo and download it. The first time you start the app it'll ask you to link an account. Enter your details again and you can now start recording using the button that appears on the screen. Remember, your iPhone's microphone will hear you like an ordinary microphone, you don't have to get close to it.

Record your Audioboo and then hit 'Publish' on your iPhone. Audioboo does the rest. If you've selected the link between Audioboo and Twitter or Facebook or both, then an automatic Tweet and/or Facebook entry that you've uploaded some audio will go out on your behalf. (Check whether these automatic notifications are on, otherwise you'll find a couple of thousand Twitter followers will be directed to an audio of you saying 'Test audioboo for social networking book...oh bugger, how do I turn this thing off?' or words to that effect. I've, er, got this friend who did that.)

Audioboo is great because the sound quality is reasonable and you can upload things really quickly. It's a nightmare, on the other hand, because you can only use it if you have an iPhone and frankly it's not worth changing your phone for the sake of a single application. More flexible is iPadio, another free application, the best feature of which is that you don't have to download anything, it's all done at their end. You go to www.ipadio.com and click on 'Register', fill in the usual boxes to set up an account, then log in. You'll be given a number you can call, and when you call you'll be asked for the PIN that is on the screen. Then start talking. Again, you can link this to your Twitter and Facebook account so that when you have a coughing fit and want to dial in again, iPadio will tweet and Facebook the fact that you've been online. There are options to have group calls so you can blog interviews.

When you go to your iPadio account and select 'My phlogs' (a phlog being a phone blog, naturally), you'll find a piece of code you can put onto your website. This places your phlog on your website, with a picture if you've uploaded one. So, you phone someone from your mobile and upload it (there can be all manner of reasons for doing this as long as your customers will be interested), you upload it and those who are following you on Twitter or reading your Facebook updates see it immediately; when you're back in the office you blog it so that your other contacts see it too.

Perhaps you want your customers to hear from a new supplier, or perhaps some of your e-newsletter or blog would work better heard than read.

Location-based social media

A number of phones can work out where they are by simple triangulation with their signal masts. This becomes useful when a social media user wants to connect with people locally and there are a number of small network apps that will let you chat with people in your immediate area.

More importantly, people will use social media-style applications to find a restaurant or a cinema. This is very significant if you run either of those establishments, so make sure you're registered with as many directories and listings services as possible. Urbanspoon.com has listings of restaurants in Birmingham, Edinburgh, Glasgow, London and Manchester and you can get your site listed through its website. People can then find a restaurant on the website alongside professional and amateur reviews, and they can also find it through the free Urbanspoon app on their iPhone if they're in the vicinity. Likewise, Flixster.com is a movie review site that includes information on where a film might be showing. There are ratings by fellow site members and links to professional reviews, and there is an iPhone app that finds where someone is and tells them where their nearest cinema showing a particular film is located. If you run a cinema you need to be on that site.

There is a lot going on with social media on the move, and as long as the smartphone continues to be the default phone of choice for many it's going to seem increasingly unnatural to restrict your networking to the time you're sitting at your desk. For anyone who spends significant time outside the office but still wants to take advantage of social networking, a mobile device to handle it is a must.

Action points

Thinking matter

1. Do you spend a lot of time outside the office?

2. Are you aware of any missed business opportunities due to your unavailability?

3. Do you carry a mobile phone and do you use email on the move? If your answer is 'yes', should your social networking activity really be any different?

Do list

- Upgrade your phone and change to a model that has a client for Twitter, LinkedIn or whichever social network you want to use.

- Download the client and install it.

- Get networking on the move!

7 COME TOGETHER

If you've read through this book (with the possible exception of Chapter 3) you'll have a number of things at your disposal. You'll know how to take advantage of social networks when you're receiving rather than sending out information, about monitoring your brand's performance, about responding to customer criticisms and about using social networking to turn a bad situation around when you're actually remaining fairly passive. As early as Chapter 1 I started talking about your need for an objective or desired outcome: here's where you build it into the structure of your business.

You'll also understand by now where the key public social networks are on the web and how to find them and get involved. You'll have a good grasp of who's doing what, so if you're selling to pensioners you won't be marketing on Bebo; if you're looking at an audience for leisure products you probably won't be approaching too many people on LinkedIn. You will, I hope, have an idea of who's offering what and why you want to become involved, as well as how to make sure people can find you, or at least that you stand a fighting chance. You'll also have had a look at text-only social networking, and you'll have considered whether you need to be networking on the move, why and how.

That only leaves one thing to do: put it into a business plan.

Business plans: a primer

You may have grown your business haphazardly, bit by bit, particularly in a recession. If so, this section is for you. On the other hand, if you have studied business, done a course and see business planning as second nature, I'd skip the next couple of pages.

If you've never had to ask for external finance, you might never have had to put together a business plan. It's basically a road map of where you're going to go, where the money is expecting to come from and how you're going to achieve it. It will include sections on budgets, on people, on market research (of which you'll have done plenty), on the requirements of the business and of course on cash flow.

There are different sorts of business plans depending on who you're addressing. If you're putting together a plan so you know where the business is going and how it's doing, that's a plan for you and your colleagues. If you're trying to impress on the tax authorities that you're highly unlikely to pull into massive profit any time now, that's another kind of plan, and the subject of another book by someone with vastly different expertise! If you're looking for external investment, clearly the plan will be full of growth and profit and should also focus on some sort of exit point for everybody so you can all walk away millionaires.

For our purposes we're focusing only on the first of those sorts of plan. You've read this far, so you're interested in social networking. That's fine. Now we look at how you fit it into the rest of your business.

Budgets

Many books on social networks – indeed, many websites and online tutorials – make a great deal of how much you can achieve for nothing. Social networking costs zippo, nada, nowt. You'll get a whole load of customers for nothing.

This is hogwash. Let me qualify that. The direct cost associated with putting your profile about on a social network is usually nothing. But the overall effort has to be resourced properly if it's going to do anything at all for your business. You may need new people to keep your social media activities up to date. You need to ask yourself who's going to be responsible for this (and who isn't: more on that later) and where the money's going to come from. Remember, if you have different budgets for different elements of the business:

- IT won't want to pay for it. It's not technically IT, as it doesn't involve the procurement or maintenance of hardware or software.

- Sales won't want to pay for it because they're overstretched already (sales always think they're unique in this), and until it's proven to be bringing money in they won't take it seriously.

- Marketing: oh come on, you've been taking chunks out of the marketing budget ever since the credit crunch started, maybe even before.

I can't tell you where the budget needs to come from in your business, but it needs to come from somewhere. Social networking can be expensive and it's labour intensive: is it something you can actually justify? You need to decide that independently, but there are precedents to suggest doing so might not be a bad idea. Almost a decade before writing this book I was editor of something called *The E-Commerce Handbook*, which aimed to help businesses that were starting to trade electronically. One of the distinctive features about e-commerce was that in its infancy a lot of businesses didn't take it all that seriously, and if a customer or prospect sent an email inquiry they'd be lucky if they had a reply within a week. Companies are no longer naive enough to assume they can get away with this kind of behaviour in e-commerce, but they revert to it when a customer comes in via a blog comment or a Facebook group. Same point, newer medium.

Projections

Another element that needs to be in the plan is some sort of projection of what being part of a social network is going to do for your company. In the section above I focused on costs and where the money is going to come from (usually at someone else's expense), which can seem rather negative.

The flipside of this is building the cash that's going to come from social networking into your projection. At this stage it's only fair to say: be conservative, be realistic, temper your expectations. Remember when you started your first business and how the potential market was worth millions so if you could just get one percent of that you'd get rich, but then only a fraction of the potential market turned up and you had to do something active to get further attention? Social media is the same. The hype says that Twitter is great for marketing because it had 7 million (according to Nielsen Online) users by February 09. True though this is, they're not all going to see your Tweets. Ashton Kutcher, who was able to entice people with a snap of Demi Moore in her underwear, barely scraped a million users – you're probably neither a movie star nor married to one, so you won't get that sort of attention.

Warning!

Many people will tell you there are ways of adding thousands of followers on Twitter every day if you use their methods. Generally these methods involve harvesting loads of names from unsecured websites, or finding people who have decided to follow all of their followers automatically. You don't know anything about any extra followers you might manage to get or whether they're going to spend any money with you – or whether they're going to write you off as a spammer and block you, so that even if they might otherwise have bought from you, they won't now. Avoid these 'get lots of followers quickly' merchants.

The projections that you've got to feed into your cash flow projection at first need to be pessimistic. Revenue from social networking is going to be slow, and it's likely to be pennies at first.

There are things you can do about this, of course. Suppose you do what Glasses Direct did a while back with its Twitter account: offer to give a free pair of prescription sunglasses to whoever comes up with the best reason for having them. Within minutes, the MD's tweet had been repeated by tens of people and forwarded to thousands of potential customers by their online friends and acquaintances, not in a sales-like way but in a 'this is fun and you might just get something worthwhile out of it' sort of way.

OK, I'm biased. I won. I'll tell you what, though. I've had nothing but polite service and no pressure at all to buy any more glasses from the company. I have no doubt that the whole thing spreading virally through Twitter will have earned it a load of new viewers to the website and many new customers as a result. And a mention in this book, come to think of it, although the company didn't know I was writing this at the time.

You can do similar things through Facebook and the other media, but be realistic about how many of these efforts will lead to actual sales. Whatever you do don't give up; just remember that in spite of the direct and almost intimate nature of the contact you're making with your prospects, they're still the same cynics who won't want to rise to every ad pitch they're sent. Make what you say fun and infectious and it'll catch on, and you might find you get new people following you to see what you do next.

Overall, a slow build of sales needs to go into your spreadsheet. You need to revisit this depending on how your performance actually balances out. Here's a little experiment for people still wondering whether social networking is worth doing: draw up a spreadsheet based on your competitor having social networking capacity when you don't. Once you've started to posit an exodus of your more technically minded customers, you'll probably agree it's worth doing.

Workload

If you've decided which part of your organization is going to pay for your social networking efforts and your sales projections justify continuing, you next want to think about how much work it's going to take for you and your staff. Note I'm talking about how much work it's *going* to take, not how much it *could* take.

Let's take a hypothetical example. You're a musical instrument retailer, you're web savvy and if someone wants something obscure you'll be able to find it for them. A woman joins your Facebook group and starts talking about antique harpsichords. During the exchange it becomes apparent that she's very interested in the subject, and she starts sending you private messages instead of public ones. This is fine and in no way an intrusion, it's no worse than sending someone an email.

(That said, private messages might not suit you. One or two of the TV presenters on Twitter decline to do the private message thing because their objective is to get loads of people involved and talking. You don't have to be a TV personality to have that as your aim.)

The messages continue for a fair while. They're no longer drawing attention to your company's expertise in old musical instruments, because nobody can see them apart from you and your correspondent. They're certainly evidence that your other marketing has worked somewhere or that the Facebook group is drawing in enthusiasts. Nevertheless, at some stage it becomes apparent that keen though the correspondent is, she simply isn't going to buy an antique harpsichord from you, restored or otherwise. You're not reaching specifics and you're not approaching closure on the sale. The options are:

● Keep on corresponding: you're enjoying it and for all you know your correspondent has friends who'll spend a fortune.

● Try to get the discussion moved back to the public area: you accept that you might never get a sale out of this person, but you might pull some other sales through by talking to her. Better still, she might attract other enthusiasts who'll keep talking and make your Facebook page engaging without you having to do much except take the swear words out. If you want to.

● Ignore her: if she were turning up regularly at your retail premises and never buying anything you'd soon learn to disregard her.

Of those options I'd probably plump for the second, but I'd have to say it would be difficult. You need to ask yourself the following questions:

- How much time is my company spending on this person?

- How much is this costing us financially?

- What else could we be doing with this time and money?

The answer might well be that you're not doing this for a hobby as so many people do, and that you can't justify continuing the conversation. Beware, though; customers will have different expectations of your Facebook site as compared to a company website simply because it's in a different medium.

A well-known movie franchise set in space – there are plenty to choose from – ran a blog for collectors during a specific promotion. When the promotion was finished the company said that was it, thanks for coming, the blog is now closing; and the fans went into uproar. Eventually the original site relented and, in a variation of the second solution above, handed the running of the blog over to the fans. The end result was that everyone was happy. The fans were enjoying themselves and unconsciously getting loads more people to the website. The company therefore had, suddenly, a lot of new workers bringing new customers in without thinking about it; although you can be certain someone from the company was still overseeing that site to check for libels and inaccuracies. It won't always work out like that, but the option's worth considering.

Whatever you decide to do, check the likely workload and balance it against the skill set you need to have within your company, or need to bring in.

Skill sets

Do you have an established webmaster in your organization or do you outsource that to someone else? If the answer is that you do it in-house, you should find that adding social networking isn't that onerous, as the webmaster will want to bring their skills up to date anyway. Social networking is something they're likely to take for granted, as we'll see later in this chapter.

Probably the most important thing to remember if you're recruiting someone, or auditing your existing in-house skills, is that you're looking for someone who can communicate. This isn't a technology job. Clearly, someone who is completely technophobic isn't going to help you at all, but someone whose skills are purely technical is going to do a great deal to hold you back.

It's worth looking at what people are actually advertising for when they're searching for someone to manage an online community and engage in social networking. A scan of a number of recruitment sites and newspapers suggests the elements include:

- Commissioning contributors. Don't ever assume that people will contribute to your social network without prompting; they might need a lot of encouragement first. They also need to be skilled in writing copy themselves.

- Participating in the online community when it starts. Your organi-zation must be seen to be participating, otherwise you're doing little more than creating some sort of fan system, most probably in a field that doesn't actually attract that many fans.

- Planning and structuring an online community. This is going to involve deciding whether you want to build your own community on your own site, whether something like Facebook would be appropriate, whether Twitter is going to work better for you than a blog.

The person will also need a lot of imagination. Writing a blog entry or stimulating some discussion is easy as a one-off, but will the candidate for the job still be generating ideas by the end of his or her first year?

Quick horror story: someone was talking to me about this sort of position a while ago. They were offering money, so I was interested. It didn't come to anything, partly because they felt – fair cop – that I was a writer rather than a manager, but partly because they felt someone working away from their premises would end up treated like, I quote, a 'second-class citizen'. If I ever write a book on how to demonstrate a complete misunderstanding of social networking, that's going on page 1.

Salary is going to be a sticking point for many. Market forces will inevitably dictate what the job is worth if you're recruiting afresh and the best place to look is the *Guardian*, which for decades has had one of the best media recruitment pages in the UK, published every Monday as part of the Media supplement. Do benchmark your salary and package by looking in there. Do also call agencies who are recruiting in the area pretending to be a candidate and ask what the job pays, they're used to it and they do the same to their competition.

Some kinds of people shouldn't be running your social networking operation, although all too often they end up doing just that. Many of the following examples of people who shouldn't handle the task are drawn from real life:

- The overworked owner/manager who already has too much to do (that'll account for a number of readers, I expect).

- The overworked cynic who hasn't really bought into this new social networking stuff.

- The office junior who hasn't yet got the hang of who does what, so can't handle the customer issues.

- The PR in an outsourced office who is completely outside of the day-to-day running of the business and who, no matter how much goodwill they have, can't help with a given problem.

These people will damage your business's reputation rather than enhance it. They won't mean to, they just will.

In-house or outsourced?

The decision whether you should handle your social networking in-house or outsource it will depend on a number of things:

- Do you already use a PR company? If so, they might well have economies of scale and in-house skills for incorporating social networking not only into the package of services they offer, but into a coherent strategy for your business.
- Is your PR company (if you have one) itself marketing through these networks?
- Do you have spare manpower in the office and people who are already on the social networking sites?
- Do you want to test market, as in try social networking and see how it goes rather than commit to it as a policy full time? If so, an independent freelance to whom you're under no obligation will be more cost-effective in the short term than a staff member; staff might be cheaper in the longer term as they accept less money in exchange for job security.

If you're doing this for the first time, and I assume that's why you're reading this book, then you'll clearly need to put some metrics in place to measure how effective your use of social media is. Like other branches of PR and communication, it can be difficult to quantify. Too many people think they've failed in these areas because they have given themselves no way of telling whether they've succeeded.

It's useful to adopt a checklist mentality. You might want to work out a formula based on:

- Investment

- Personnel

- Time

- New equipment

- Desired outcome

- Achieved outcome

And of course you need to revisit your desired output by checking it against the achieved output. It could be that your market is incredibly suited to a social networking approach to marketing. It may be that your staff or recruited social networking implementor has an incredible flair for putting hilarious videos together, and interest in your services has increased dramatically as a result. This clearly means revising your forecasts upward instead of downward.

Try putting a table together like this, for starters:

Network	Person allocated	Time/cash	Desired outcome	Actual
MySpace				
Twitter				
Blellow				

You should soon get an idea of whether your plans are bearing fruit.

Once again, be careful. Social networking can have an effect on other areas of your business. Take the phenomenally successful American site willitblend.com. It consists mainly of a set of videos about blenders; as it happens they aren't hosted on YouTube, but there's no reason you shouldn't do something similar and use the YouTube bandwidth. It's a blender company's website. So far, so dull. Except it's aware of how dull the product could be, so the owner, Blendtec, has put together some extremely silly videos to see whether a number of products will survive in a blender. Blendtec hit some sort of high when Apple launched the iPhone and instead of talking about the product the producers put one in a blender and turned it into grey powder. This went round on Twitter and Facebook very quickly indeed, and a load of people used ordinary email to send it to their friends. But did it make me any more inclined to buy a blender?

Suppose it had encouraged me to do just that. Suppose you were also making something like a blender and had a similar idea, and the whole thing took off in the same way and customers were swayed towards your brand more than any other. Suppose you needed extra credit lines to make up the volumes. And you hadn't put this into your business plan, and the bank, uncomfortable with your lack of prescience about the quantities you'd be selling, decided to say 'no'.

Years ago I attended a business start-up course and the adviser from the bank was very clear: if people were overtrading and growing too quickly, this was a cause for concern and there was no guarantee that they would be granted a financial facility if their order book suggested their capacity had reached breaking point.

Increases in orders are good, of course, but only as long as the rest of the business can be managed in such a way that it keeps pace. Social networking is a cheap and efficient way of test marketing and if your tests suggest it's going to go ballistic, then you can go to the bank before you need extra credit rather than after. Don't sacrifice quality control (ever!), don't slack off on continuing to check new customers for creditworthiness if you work on invoice rather than on a cash basis, keep all of those sanity checks in place as you would for any other customer and you should be fine.

The trick is to keep in mind always that this is one aspect of your business, but that it needs to fit in with the rest of it. Too many companies think of social networking as a new thing and therefore ring-fence it completely. If it's integrated into the business plan at the earliest possible stage, it becomes significantly easier to manage than if it's rationalized much later.

Pulling it together and a sanity check

Here's the big secret that no business expert ever tells you: in real life, all the planning and everything you do on paper only goes so far. Ask someone who's a small business owner when they last looked at their business plan and you'll get a very mixed response. People don't always plan and it's not always necessary.

Zoe Brewer

Take Zoe Brewer, joint owner of the Elmfield Hotel in Devon. She and her husband set up the hotel and use social networks to publish various events at it; her husband was head of new media at a record company and she also worked for a new media-savvy company before. They host events and publicize them through Facebook and Twitter and they have a blog on their website; although they don't track exactly who makes bookings after looking at what. In fact, sometimes they find their net savviness works against them. Brewer explains: 'We get people ringing up for a brochure and we tell them we don't have one, we have a website, and they say they don't have access to the Internet.' She acknowledges that this could work against them when it comes to certain customers.

The social media stuff has always been there in the plan without having specific resources allocated. 'We're social media fluent as individuals so it just comes as second nature – I sit down and check my emails, check Twitter, go on Facebook.' 90 percent of the business comes through people looking at the website, but Brewer doesn't make any specific claims about how many of them have read the blog, received a tweet or checked the Facebook pages.

In many ways the Brewers are ahead of many businesses in this respect, and their method will undoubtedly become the norm. Once people are used to social networking without thinking about it, they will no more plan specific resources around it than they would for writing letters and answering the phone. It'll just be natural. While there is a learning curve to negotiate, while there is a culture gap that suggests staff won't take a sales lead coming in through Blellow as seriously as someone walking in through the door, it probably needs a little more work. I have no doubt that in future editions of this book – maybe not the very next – this will be the first section outside the listings to be altered dramatically.

Policies

At the risk of sounding dull and boring, you'll also need to put some policies in place to control just how much your staff use social networking sites. These are the kinds of things that can happen when people are using social media in a cack-handed or unwise manner:

- In May 2009, a teacher in Lanarkshire was being investigated by her employers because she was tweeting things about her pupils. This was against school policy; in this instance it would have meant students were able to find out just how disillusioned she was with them, how amusing she found the one with Asperger's… you get the picture.

- In the same year a woman secured a job with computer networking specialist Cisco, and tweeted that she only had to decide which she'd hate more, the commute or the job. She had a pretty prompt response from a Cisco senior who also tweeted, explaining that they did understand about social media and if she didn't want the job she simply needn't turn up.

- A US Governor tweeted about how the state he was visiting was a hell-hole and a dive, and wondered how the people living there didn't kill themselves. You'll have guessed what's coming, but just to confirm; they saw it, it hit the local press, and he was appropriately embarrassed.

There was also an airline whose marketing staff set up a Twitter account for a laugh, insulting customers small-minded enough to take blog entries seriously. This was bad news for the airline and the Twitter account was closed down immediately. Even worse was the pizza company that found a couple of employees on YouTube applying various nasal fluids to the pizzas for a laugh...and sharing it with the world.

The airline has been tight-lipped about the fate of its employees who were making so free and easy with their company name on Twitter (and indeed using the company's logo); the pizza company was perfectly up front about dismissing the employees immediately and consulting the police because of food safety issues. Those are really straightforward instances. Less so is the overenthusiastic employee who blogs or tweets future developments, not because he or she wants to ruin the company but out of genuine excitement about what it's doing for customers. What you need is some sort of policy about acceptable use.

This would cover:

● What employees may or may not do on social networks in the company's name.

● What they may do in their own time in networking terms. Nobody should want to be too draconian about this, and clearly someone's own time really is their own; however, there's nothing wrong with reinforcing the idea that bringing the company into disrepute is a sackable offence in any medium, and commercial confidences are confidential!

● Consider also the effect social networking can have on productivity in your organization. I've emphasized a number of times that it can take over and become a bit of an obsession, and I'd really recommend that you limit employees in some way. Again, being draconian won't win you any friends and if you don't mind people making the odd phone call home or to book a theatre ticket, then a bit of Facebooking isn't going to harm anyone either. There's no reason not to allow social use of the computer only during certain hours, though.

Check the policy you do put in place with the company's lawyers, and make sure you explain that there is a sanction for disregarding it. As long as you're not being unreasonable, and as long as you're not dealing with Members of Parliament, there shouldn't be any problem.

If you don't have a policy

One company had been getting a rough press for the very simple reason that it was well known the head honcho absolutely hated journalists. You can imagine he was less than delighted when blogging, Facebook and Twitter made it easy for just about anyone to publish their own words about his organization and its services. The organization caused a little consternation when it made its contempt for various bloggers apparent in a company statement but never mind – everyone drops clangers.

Then a Twitter account appeared in the company's name. A website picked up the story and called the marketing director, who confirmed there was indeed a Twitter account going up, to engage the public. But when people looked at the Twitter account, it responded to everyone who posted anything with an insult, calling them a retard or a saddo, or whatever. Insulting customers, a director confirming the site was genuine...this was dynamite for the press, so a report appeared immediately on the website of one of the national newspapers.

Within less than an hour a load of us had blogged this as an example of how not to use social media. Meanwhile, the marketing director presumably saw the blog and came down like a ton of whatsit on the individual in the organization who'd put the site up. An overzealous, laddish sales executive was responsible: he'd used the company's name and logo but this wasn't the official Twitter account at all. The website that had the director's confirmation of its authenticity amended the story so it said there was an imposter out there pretending to be this organization on Twitter, the national newspaper took its coverage down and the Twitter account was scrapped. The whole incident blew over within hours, luckily.

The company is still not on Twitter, presumably working on the basis of 'once bitten...,' which is a shame because it could still usefully engage with its clients, bypassing the press who find its boss antagonistic in the extreme.

The week before that I'd been speaking at an event in London on social media and someone had asked me: what do you do about people who abuse social media and make unwanted mentions of the company for which they work? I told her the answer was quite simple;

you invoke the contractual clause in people's employment that says that if they bring their company into disrepute they're dismissed immediately.

Why people assume there are special rules for new media I don't know: normal business rules apply. You might already be thinking of revisiting some of your contracts for your employees, which is good.

Another question came up at the same event and it was more tricky to manage. If a colleague or employee is deliberately bad-mouthing you on a blog, Facebook or Twitter, then fine, you can take action against them. In this instance, a PR manager in a technology company had a more complex issue. Her developers were really, really keen on the gadgets they made: which was great, if you're in PR then the spokesperson meaning what they say about how neat the devices they make are is a brilliant thing. The thing is, they were so excited they couldn't resist blogging about them. On their own personal blogs. They didn't say 'this is the company view', they didn't use the logo, just their own names – but they would pre-announce stuff that wasn't officially out. 'We're developing functions A, B and C into the next version of product D,' they'd say. The person whose job it was to manage the launches and keep new items away from prying eyes had to find some way of calming these people's enthusiasm and towing the company line without appearing like a control freak. She loved their keenness but hated the fact that the buying public wouldn't now buy the current gadgets because they knew about the stuff that was coming in the near future.

Action points

Thinking matter

1. Are you already being represented online without actually knowing it?

2. Is there someone in your organization or a communications company you employ that's already equipped to promote you through social networking?

3. Do you have an acceptable use policy?

Do list

- Set up an acceptable use policy for social networking immediately.

- Identify the most likely social networkers in your company.

- Evaluate the market and set some objectives before beginning your networking activity.

8 WHERE IS THIS GOING?

Traditionally an author finishes a book like this by telling you what to expect next. There's crystal ball gazing, there are words of wisdom. The thing is, technology moves quickly. Sometimes people go for a particular innovation, sometimes they don't.

Let me explain with an example. In the mid-1990s, not so long ago, Apple Computer was a computer company. It still is, but it's more now. In the late 1990s a company called Diamond started making a lot of noise (pun intended) about a gadget called the Diamond Rio. This was something they called an MP3 player. You could 'rip' music onto it and play it. Diamond didn't have the marketing clout that Apple had and it lacked the sheer design panache, so Apple picked up the idea, made it look like a neat product to own and an easier one to operate (reasoning that if people didn't have to learn it they'd just get on with it) and before very long Apple was a music machine store and seller of online tunes as well as a computer company. In the mid-1990s nobody would have seen this coming.

Likewise, even when blogging started (and putting your thoughts down on a website and bringing in links, pictures and anything else you might want sounded a mighty strange idea in theory before we'd all seen one), if someone had said you would soon be able to produce a sort of mini-blog, severely limited in character count, you'd have said they were crazy. Only I've just described Twitter. It sounds like an unlikely success story.

Outside the computer field there was the Filofax: remember that? Basically paper put into a nice folder. Everybody had one, but it was only a simple idea and hardly revolutionary. Ditto an innovation in the 1970s, Sony's Walkman. Everyone raved about it, but they'd had cassette players and earphones for ages. This wasn't so much new stuff as a new combination of existing stuff, hailed as a major breakthrough.

So here I am trying to work out what's going to be the next major wave of social networking. Tricky. Part of me wants to say it'll be something we've already seen and failed to recognize. Someone, somewhere, will spot what fits together and just do it.

There are a few pointers available if you care to look for them. I've adopted one in this book: the inclusion of Blellow in Chapter 3's listing of the great and the good in social media is a bit of a flier, since it's a very new company that started while I was writing this book. Whereas it might take off and become the business world's Twitter, equally it might not. If it doesn't, it won't be the technology that's wrong – sometimes the market does something unexpected; opts for VHS rather than Betamax, adopts a micro-blogging service that people who don't use think is a waste of time.

Look at what's happening in the search engine space. When I discussed search engine optimization I offered some pointers to what you might do to make your website search engine friendly. Half way through writing that chapter, Wolfram Alpha joined in the fray and received a huge amount of attention. It operates differently from its competition and offers answers rather than a set of links when you enter a question – or, more likely if your query isn't completely America-centric, it tells you it doesn't know what to do with the information you've entered. Is that going to change the nature of search engine behaviour? At this stage I can honestly say I have no idea. Google looks pretty unseatable as the lord of all searches at the moment, but 10 years ago so did AltaVista, Excite! and all the other directories people were using. In late 2008 another pretender to the search engine throne, Cuil.com, was launched; it hasn't yet caught light as a force in the market, but it may yet do so. Again, its founders say it behaves slightly differently from the other search engines available. Half of me says 'they would, wouldn't they', the other half says they may be right.

Then in the week of this book's deadline – no, really – Bing. Not the singer, not Matthew Perry's surname in Friends, not the PG Wodehouse character or the old email address of Stephen Fry who undoubtedly named himself after the Wodehouse character, but Microsoft's Bing. Launching to developers in the US, Bing is Microsoft's new approach to web searches. On the Bing.com website the company says: 'We took a new approach to go beyond search to build what we call a decision engine. With a powerful set of intuitive tools on top of a world-class search service, Bing will help you make smarter, faster decisions. We included features that deliver the best results, presented in a more organized way to simplify key tasks and help you make important decisions faster.'

I have no idea what that's going to add up to in practical terms, but it sounds as though it could be radical (or marketing waffle). And although Microsoft hasn't cracked the search engine market previously any more than Google has threatened Microsoft's market dominance in the office productivity suite market, you underestimate Bill Gates' marketing capacity at your peril. The rules on getting your site, blog or tweets noticed could be about to change, big time.

If that wasn't enough of a change, in the same week Google announced a project called Google Wave. Part of it is a development of email. Google describes it as email as if it had been invented now – so it's easier to put bits of media like video or sound in, and when two people emailing each other are both online it switches to instant messaging instead. It also contains event planning.

Why is this important to us? Because technology takes unexpected turns. Because Twitter wasn't planned as a social network tool in which people could talk to each other but as something people could use to make simple announcements. Google Wave will help people collaborate, it involves messaging and multimedia elements and it could – just could – take one of those unexpected turns and revolutionizing social media as a concept, if it can become one-to-many communication rather than simply one-to-one or collaboration within a workgroup.

Twitter burned slowly at first, but its ascent to dominance happened in the space of a few months. Is it going to continue as the leading social medium for so many people? Again, that's difficult to tell. The very simplicity that earned it so many plaudits and admirers could start to pall. A number of bloggers are starting to talk things up as the 'next Twitter', although whether they're serious or merely worried that they'll miss the next biggie when it does come along is anybody's guess. There will be repercussions from Facebook's acquisition of Friendfeed and Facebook has now released 'Facebook Lite'. Nobody knows how all of this will turn out.

All of this is my way of breaking it to you gently that I have no idea what the next major trend will be: whether you should be preparing for everyone abandoning Google and opting for Bing or Wolfram Alpha; whether Cuil.com will start directing you to Blellow instead of Twitter for your updates. I'd certainly guess that whatever mechanism evolves for bringing together your various different feeds will do well. Tweetdeck's bringing Facebook information in has been a good step in that direction, but it's an add-on rather than a new network or a revolutionary way of working.

Maybe there won't *be* a revolutionary new way of working. Maybe the answer to the question about what's coming next was buried in the first chapter of this book, in which I spoke about my early days networking socially with Cix, CompuServe, AOL and other facilities like those. Perhaps things haven't changed as radically as all that. Perhaps there's one constant that we shouldn't overlook in all of these social networks: people.

People will keep communicating. Ever since the first magazine launched its first letters page, people have wanted to make their presence felt and feed back into things when they are presented with information or offered a viewpoint. We react. All that's changed is that we can all make our voices heard rather than only one or two of us on a letters page that's limited by space and the editor's choice. And it can be an ongoing conversation rather than a one-way monologue (even a letters page offers only the briefest of opportunities to make one comment).

People will harness whatever technology they can in order to communicate. Twitter wasn't about communicating at first, it was about making announcements. The Internet itself was largely a series of brochures initially, then blogs came along and turned it into a debating ground. Now it feels wrong when a news story online hasn't got a space for comments.

It's this element of which you can take advantage. People want to engage with each other whether they're online or not. They may well want to engage with you.

Look closely at the product or service you offer and think it through. Look at the customers you have and the ones you want to gain. Is social media right for you? If so, then by all means look through Chapter 3 and decide which of the various offerings is best for you and business plan it in as in Chapter 7. Also look on the web. Some of the players I've discussed might conceivably have gone away.

However, the principle of people wanting to engage somehow will not change. The name on the tin might be Twitter, or Facebook, or Blellow, or something completely different, but you can be certain the idea will still be around. And the planning, the resources, the motivation of an online community, the balance between spending time on this compared to the likely return on your investment: all these stay the same.

These are the skills you'll need to make social networking work for you. Remember the 'social' bit, so no hard sell: think Tupperware Party rather than door-to-door hawking. Remember to give people a reason to come back to you even if they're not spending money each time. Remember an engagement is two-way, but also remember you've got a living to make and you're not doing this as a hobby, it's a business, so you do need a financial return of some sort.

Get social networking right with the right business and you should start to see results in the form of hard cash arriving very quickly. You'll also see people enthused and recommending your product and service without your having to pay for massive extra publicity. Make it part of the mix – don't mistake it for a substitute for traditional marketing but part of it, a new facet – and it will be incredibly cost-effective.

Good luck!

LIST OF
DEFINITIONS
IN THIS BOOK